The "Centering" of America

Marc L. Lanoue, Ph. D.

ISBN: 979-8-89412-912-9

CONTENTS

PREFACE

The pages that follow describe how I currently view the scene on the American landscape. The description developed involves politics, but also draws from perspectives related to social issues such as the economy, healthcare, and general rights, all of which people can find commentary on the evening news and in other periodic literature. My comments primarily stem from these limited periodicals, especially *The Week* magazine, which attempts to encapsulate several viewpoints pertaining to a specific topic, accomplished weekly in 40 pages. I have also drawn from books that I have read, particularly on matters pertaining to medicine and healthcare. My own experiences in life have also formed me as happens also with others, attempting to draw metaphors that can help me at least to appreciate and understand what is going on in our country and world at large and how these matters affect not only myself, but others as well.

I also draw from some of the movies that I have seen, which I use to further some metaphors, but also to gain insight through them, which I believe offers a sense of the reality that is unfolding. These movies are not necessarily Oscar winners, but are instead films that spoke to me. Some of the courses that I have recently taken as well as my own experiences impact what I develop within the 12 chapters that follow.

In other words, this is an eclectic blend of materials that have affected my own experience of current events, but also how I view those events from a broader perspective. I have moved three times in the last eighteen months, attempting to find work, which has made me wonder about economic matters, especially obtaining a job with benefits, as well as how I will contribute to society in a meaningful way: Both for my own benefit (fulfillment) and that of society at large. In this I believe that I am like most people in attempting to recognize where I am now, but also projecting where I want to be—to the extent that I can—and how such decisions can impact my quality of life and that of others.

The political landscape seems rather bleak these days, given the limited options for leadership. Nonetheless, my comments below attempt to find a path through the minefield of political and public opinions that currently exist in our country and in our world. I am a firm believer that if we as a nation do not address our own problems in an effective way, then we will be limited in our ability to deal with international issues that develop and affect us, though these matters are interconnected. Our interconnectedness, it seems to me, is key for finding a way through the tangled web that we have woven out of technology, security, politics, and so much more.

Transcendence in all quarters, I believe, can offer a perspective to help both the individual and the collective to come to mutually agreeable ends, since I believe that these two dominant views pervade our current dialogues, making them acrimonious. Nonetheless, recognizing the heart of the problem can lead to solutions. This is the hope of the remarks below, though they represent only a beginning. Hope needs to have a plan to be effective. It is my hope that these words can offer some kind of assistance toward realizing a plan of action that will help us to address the complex, multifaceted nature of the issues that face us today.

1 THE LABYRINTH

I visited the Delaware Art Museum near where I live. Housed within its walls are works by various artists. But when I left the museum itself, I followed the path to the parking lot which was circuitous, but which ended in a labyrinth, housed behind a man-made hill. A labyrinth is a maze of sorts, whose path is unclear, though its end is always in view. It was hard to trod the path this day, because leaves blanketed the rocks demarcating the path, where a set of rocks provided a boundary where the person following the path needed to take a turn. I was able to get to the center of the path, which is the purpose of the labyrinth, but the entire structure, which was about the size of an infield for a baseball diamond, was deliberately built to house this feature. This construct can serve as a model for appreciating one's path of life, recognized in both secular and religious terms.

The Path

How people's lives progress is full of various events that contribute more or less to one's development. Some figure prominently, like someone's first kiss or first job. They are often first experiences in one's life. These events can make a lasting impression on someone. What a person had for dinner on a given night might not matter in the long run, unless that person received very good or bad news during the meal. In the instant when someone learns special news, perhaps this draws the person into a sense of recognition of every aspect of the moment, adding to how it is recalled.

Some people can remember smells, tastes, feelings, or particular facts that, in any other experience of the same event, might deliver a different response. However, more is operative than "meets the eye," which means that things are happening in the background that cause a person to remember such an event in this kind of detail. Typically, first-responders question witnesses to crimes or accidents as soon after the event as possible, since the vivid nature of the experience can lessen over time and details can fade. Nonetheless, we experience events that may have no impact or those that have great impact, changing our lives forever, but we also experience everything in between at various stages in our lives. Our openness to these experiences determines how or whether we change as human beings. This is what we call "growth."

Growth

Growth is the learning process, which may be experienced in huge ways or more subtle ones. Sometimes we are the actors, but oftentimes we are acted upon by our surroundings. I once read in a magazine someone's claim that he or she had not chosen to be born or made choices in various arenas of life; things were chosen for her. I'm not so sure that the nature of choice is so black and white or cut and dry as to warrant giving it more emphasis over the general circumstances of life that we may not choose, but that still affect us. This is our path, so to speak, as we make progress in a forward direction toward some goal or not, known or unknown. Either way, the progression of life itself propels us in a forward direction, which is the positive valuation of our state of being. After all, we might say: "I took two steps forward and one step back(ward)." This is seen in terms of progress in relation to some project, but for one's state of being, progress is typically seen as pressing forward, though we may regress in our inner states.

Control

The labyrinth does have a path to its center, but the person traveling this path must have trust that those who put it together have given it a solution, so that a person is not wandering forever, which can cause frustration or other difficulties. Frustration can stem from an inability to control one's surroundings. After all, someone else laid out the plan of the labyrinth. But the willingness to suspend one’s control is part of the objective, it seems to me, in entering the labyrinth. Control is the exercise of ego-strength, one’s locus within the psyche for making choices. But when one enters a labyrinth, one gives control over to someone else. One must rely on following the rocks that delimit the path, so that the person progressing takes the correct step as indicated by the rocks. It’s rather like a ship avoiding the rocks on the sea, so that it can *not* only avoid problems, but also make progress on its journey.

Lack of Control

We tend to ignore the state of being that requires people to give over their control as though this is a lesser state of being, especially in American society. But when I ride in a car with someone else driving, I don’t view this as relinquishing control of my life or status or anything else, though some may see this circumstance in this way. “I’m putting my life in your hands” usually means that the person driving may be reckless. It is a euphemism. I admit that I have caused family members to question why they accepted for me to drive them. Nonetheless, sometimes being driven by someone else is needed, not out of a loss of control, but out of the need to take fewer cars or for a variety of reasons that do not have anything to do with control. That aspect of control, then, can be seen as a compulsion for some, which stands in the way of looking at situations in a way that is neutral rather than about something always to do with control.

I know that when I ride with others, I am able to notice more of the scenery that passes by. I have often wondered where I was when I then notice aspects of the landscape, which I missed due to concerns for maintaining safety during driving. In other words, these are different concerns that surface, where focus is one thing for a specific reason, but it need not be seen as the “be all and end all” of my existence.

Compulsions

I have several compulsions in my life, whereas others have dissipated over time. I can recall that I used to be a “clean freak” to such an extent that I made it my business to clean people’s homes—at least the areas where I stayed—so that I could feel “comfortable” staying there. I was unable to accept these locales as they were. I had to put my stamp of approval on them through some form of cleaning or ordering. I no longer use/need this compulsion to move forward, but we should not lose track of its purpose. I could not accept places or situations, so I used the act of cleaning to make that locale or situation more palatable. The cleaning served as a transitional activity so that my nervous energy associated with interacting with others or coming to a new place could go in a constructive direction. Compulsions are not "bad" per se, unless they undermine people's lives in some fashion.

I noticed once again recently that I rinse items which were headed for the recycle bin. I started doing this so that the bin would remain relatively free of items that might leave an odor if left there. But recycling requirements where I currently live are different. I continue to wash everything, but someone noticed that I was doing it, so the person questioned me. There is no purpose in the action, but I continue to do it. Such a scenario underscores the purpose of compulsions. They serve a purpose for a time, but we need to outgrow them, which signals growth in our lives.

Outgrowing Our Needs

At one time, there was a need for me to be "Mr. Clean," which is a euphemism for a clean freak in some circles. But if we follow the compulsion back, we can see that it served the purpose of handling nervous energy of various sorts, especially when company would come over—people with whom I was uncomfortable interacting. It was, then, a transitional activity, that is, an activity that helped me to cope with the presence of other people. Over time, I have dispensed with the need for this activity, which means that I became more comfortable with dealing with other people in social and other settings. I am more comfortable with myself, which makes me more comfortable with others. The two seem to work together. I have seen people take on the role of bartender or gadfly or photographer in social settings. The awkwardness of conversations with these people underscored how uncomfortable these individuals were within these situations. Over time, people can outgrow the need for these transitional activities, though not everyone does. Sometimes it takes instruction to move on from a needed behavior that became a compulsion and a helper for us to cope.

Instruction Out of Compulsion

I can recall my dread about dinner parties and receptions, where my mind would go blank in asking people questions to keep a conversation going. The awkwardness, I suppose, is what I would dread experiencing. This was the case for me, until someone pointed out that I ought to learn everything that I could about the person whom I was meeting and treat this process as a goal. Once I had finished with that goal, then I could rest easy, knowing that I could now just "coast" and ask people about themselves with no expectations. That tip about socializing has saved me ever since implementing it, so that I do not dread such social experiences anymore. It can be advantageous for people to receive instruction in emotional intelligence and social interactions, which may be common sense for some, but which is unknown to others. I recall someone saying that everyone had common sense. I corrected that person, stating that common sense meant that it was readily found, making it common, but that not everyone had it. I live within the realm of this distinction.

Compulsions and "All or Nothing" Thinking

It is difficult for people who have compulsions of various sorts to see matters in their lives clearly and objectively. This does not mean that they cannot get up in the morning and live their lives, as someone suffering from clinical depression might, which is not a compulsion, but a clinical difficulty. Instead, I am speaking of how people may view the world as originating out of only one perspective.

One night on *NBC News*, the commentator had traveled to Dartmouth College in New Hampshire to report on how that school had been dealing with the student protests related to the Israel-Hamas War. The dialogue, chaired by the president of the college herself, permitted students to voice their opinions related to this crisis, where all people were permitted to speak, and everyone's voice was presumably heard. More than a thousand students had participated at the time of the report. This is remarkable. Other colleges and universities contacted Dartmouth to find out their methodology. I found it baffling why other colleges and universities, which are meant to be bastions for the freedom of speech, needed to inquire about the nuts and bolts of a campus-wide discussion. Somehow it seems that colleges and universities have become stalwarts of unilateral statements that represent *their* positions, whereas the student body comes from other perspectives. Such stances caught these institutions of higher learning off guard.

Dartmouth's willingness to venture into this nexus zone, which was mistakenly *assumed* at Harvard and elsewhere, points to a wake-up call for these institutions. It seems that their own compulsive thinking needed to be brought out into the open, so that it could contend with itself. Those who are typically the professors and administration needed to learn some lessons, that their student body is not as homogeneous as they seem to have believed.

One student was quoted as asking whether questioning the tactics of Israel within Gaza was innately antisemitic. The question was left unanswered. All or nothing thinking would lead us to conclude that questioning any tactic used by Israel is antisemitic, yet the student's question, which I have to admit speaks as well for me, permits us to contend with important issues in ways that lead to making progress if only to appreciate where two (or more) sides are coming from in their assessments of the situation being discussed. But it is important to note that Dartmouth's experience and experiment within this discussion forum overarchingly follows the nature of the labyrinth, where the goal is understanding, but the path is unsure, set on trust as a foundation.

Trust

Dartmouth's president had to establish trust with the student body and faculty at her college, otherwise her forum could have devolved into violence and further problems. Be this as it may, her courage permitted her to provide this forum for her students, who also took a chance on trust. Trust is one of those states of being that is hard to define, but it is the underlying "energy" that is required for one person to connect (emotionally, socially, etc.) with another person. Those who have over-arching compulsions or who are socially awkward may have trouble establishing trust with other people. I know that I do. Nonetheless, Dartmouth's president took a chance, which is itself an invitation to trust, and she went with it. She could have failed miserably, but instead she succeeded to such an extent that other institutions sought her help.

Trust and Our Society

Our society has largely turned in on itself, choosing to foster bad feelings of hurt or resentment or the like, rather than taking a chance on trust of others and examining its own compulsions. On the one hand, I find that some people are as awkward as I am, so, rather than increasing awkwardness, such a realization can actually diffuse it. On the other, I find that some people are so fixated on their own compulsiveness or control of situations that they cannot see the forest for the trees. The issue that is their mainstay in life has become so all-encompassing and problematic that they use their problematic behavior as a protective armor. Instead of addressing the issue, the issue or position has become their outer identity. Who among us is able to discuss in meaningful or mature terms something that we hold is necessary for us to live, even survive? Trust is difficult to establish when we believe that our identity is under attack. This is not the lesson from the labyrinth.

Another's Guidance

The labyrinth requires the one who takes its directions to suspend one's control. This can be difficult for those who see their identity solely through their ability to control, both themselves and others. This, however, can serve to undermine trust. Of course, there was someone who designed the labyrinth, and others who built it, but the point of the labyrinth is to give over one's control to the process of walking through the labyrinth. It's about letting "the art" of the experience fall over or encompass someone. There is a trust required for such acceptance, but there is also a permission for one not to be in control—to be free from the compulsions that emanate from oneself. The energy needed to maintain such states of being could be redirected to foster a different trajectory, where we are not as fixated on protecting ourselves from others as much as we are directing ourselves outwardly, so that we connect with others. Sometimes it takes another's guidance to point us in this direction, but when everyone is so concerned with protecting themselves from others, then trust and its effects will not occur, because energy is moving in the wrong direction.

Don't get me wrong: Interior reflection is necessary for people to grow, but so is interaction with others in a manner that benefits both parties. When we practice attitudes in only one direction, we become adept in such efforts. Practicing interactions with others may feel awkward for a time, especially for introverts, but by drawing back one's identity from transitional activities (cleaning, etc.) and objects (cameras), we can meet other people in their true identities, especially in their humanity.

People who are sure of themselves, who can go with the punches that they meet in life, because they've been punched in a figurative way to hone their identity, can generally handle difficult situations with finesse and acumen. They may not "enjoy" these interactions, but they are able to rise to the occasion to address them. They put themselves out there for possible failure, but this is a winning combination, because vulnerability leading to trust is at its core. Such an action springs from a willingness to connect. This is needed if we are to look beyond our own fixations and "fix" the problems that all of us face.

Conclusion

A labyrinth is a path based within a maze. The end of the labyrinth at the Delaware Art Museum was always in sight, but the leaves occluded a clear direction to follow. Nonetheless, awareness of the rocks helped to ensure that I remained on task, which was elusive, but not without ultimate reward. The labyrinth encourages its participants to suspend their control, so that they can move forward. We examined how compulsions and being fixated on something can keep us going in circles, so that we lose track of the goal, which is always there, though hidden. Trust, too, is something that is hidden, and which takes the emergence of people's willingness to risk themselves for an uncertain outcome. This is where trust comes from. Without it, we will flounder. With it, however, we can follow the labyrinth that we call life.

Our compulsions developed because of specific circumstances. We must be willing to recognize their positive place in our lives, especially the protections that they provide or provided, but mature people appreciate when it is time to let them go and release their hold on us. Some may need instruction to move forward. Some may discern the path on their own. In whatever way, may we work toward relinquishing control, not so that we are less within ourselves, but so that, venturing out, we can become more through our connections with others, recognizing what we bring to relationships. In this way, we will recognize comfort with others and comfort with ourselves. The two are interconnected, but we often emphasize one over the other. This is not a fault, but merely a point of emphasis. In this way, however, we can appreciate our interactions and learn about ourselves. This is our objective along the labyrinth of life.

In the following chapter, we will look at "green" concerns, that is, those that involve matters involving the environment and actions that impact it. We now turn to this important topic.

2 GREEN

The sense of being "green" aligns with the sense of maintaining nature, since nature is associated with the color green. This seems an obvious connection. But I would further suggest that being green is not simply about maintaining green spaces, but also about incorporating practices and materials that ensure that the environment is not used in such an overt manner that it is destroyed or otherwise contaminated, but instead it is used responsibly, so that pollution is reduced to a minimum, but new growth for the future is also maintained. Responsibility is a concept that recognizes that there is an appropriate manner in which the environment should be used, whereas there are policies that do not lead in this direction. We cannot deal with one side of this important concern without dealing with the other, because a great deal is at stake.

The Internet and Global Links

Google, Facebook, YouTube, and other platforms now connect the world in a manner that seemed like science fiction only thirty years ago. The number of innovations technologically is staggering. These connections occur largely due to the use of computers, networks, and the Internet. The difficulties brought about by the pandemic were lessoned somewhat by the connectivity that people enjoyed in their homes through their Internet providers, but also by the computers and other devices that made use of these gateways to the outside world. This foundation made it possible for people to work from home. Zoom and other similar platforms made classroom learning and business meetings possible for people to communicate under the stressors of the pandemic. These were positive responses to a difficult situation, which continues, but it offers an alternative model to use which will probably change the workplace forever.

People are connected through the Internet with others in their communities, offices, locations in other countries, and in the world. Postings on Facebook can be accessed in seconds. This was all made possible through connectivity. But there is a cost associated with the use of so many computers and that is the energy that they require to function. We will use the example of the company, Amazon, to illustrate some of the stakes involved in the use of computers, but also maintaining a green focus in how we move forward both in the US and in other countries.

Amazon

The company, Amazon, has commercials that describe how it is going to have net-zero carbon-emissions by the year 2040. Its fleet of trucks, which I have personally seen driving around, are ubiquitous, as they deliver the goods that people order from their web-site. This is a great effort in the need for the environment to reduce emissions. Amazon's leadership stems from its place as a top seller to whom much of America appeals to obtain their goods. I do this myself.

But I was also speaking with someone very much "in the know" about "the cloud," that is, remote computing services of various sorts, which use servers that Amazon and other companies provide. Since I worked in Information Technology (IT) for around ten years, I asked if I was correct in assuming that there had to be physical storage units somewhere on the planet that would provide for the cloud to function in the way that it does. My colleague indicated that this was, in fact, true.

I'm sure that most people have been to a doctor's office or to the Department of Motor Vehicles, where they scan everything: Licenses, birth records, insurance cards, etc. Scanners digitize images of records, so that they can be kept and accessed on-line. These pictures require huge amounts of disk space, as well as highly developed algorithms to access them in real time. Use of paper is generally obsolete in these circumstances, though the paperless office has never been realized.

I have recently read that Microsoft and Amazon have been vying for contracts with the federal government to provide cloud services, which means that very large server "farms" have to be maintained in order to provide the storage capacity necessary to address the needs of the federal government, which I would surmise to be enormous.

My colleague spoke casually about "petabytes" of data, which is 1,000 terabytes, where 1 terabyte is equivalent to 1,000 gigabytes and 1 gigabyte is equivalent to 1,000 megabytes. 1,000 kilobytes are equivalent to 1 megabyte. A typical MS-Word document of one page is about 23 kilobytes. If you follow the figures, dealing with government bureaucracy will require a great deal of storage space, which I find hard to comprehend. My colleague deals with this—and more—on a daily basis. (I had to ask my colleague for a definition of petabytes.) But we need to consider the electricity that is necessary to maintain these enormous server farms, as well as the heat that they generate and the cooling that they require. These are not trivial considerations, given the amount of data that it seems that we are dealing with.

Responsibility

I believe that we should applaud Amazon's commitment to reducing its carbon emissions as well as its support of renewable energy sources. Its web-site indicates that it will purchase or provide its own renewable energy by 2025, years before its intended full implementation of this initiative. This is true leadership. But Amazon is in a unique position as one of the most profitable companies in the US and abroad. It has the capital to invest in these initiatives, which is a great thing, but what about the rest of society?

Increased Energy Consumption

Amazon is attempting to make the energy that it uses clean, meaning that it does not pollute the atmosphere by its own use of energy, which is a good undertaking. Yet, given the number of computers that are required to run cloud servers, one should be cautious about what is at stake with an increase in energy consumption. Where is the energy going to come from that produces the electricity that powers the computers and other devices, like electric cars? This is no trivial question. I am using Amazon as an example, because it is a public company, but our society is moving toward greater use of electricity even as it moves away from burning fossil fuels for energy. This is a good step toward ensuring that our society does not unnecessarily contribute to carbon emissions and other pollutants. Yet the question still exists: Where will we get the needed energy to power all of our electronic devices, which seem to be proliferating?

Other Sources of Sustainable Energy

Turbine farms, which I have witnessed both in Massachusetts and even more in California, produce electricity, which is powered by the wind. People may not appreciate the sight of such large devices on the landscape, but there can be no question that turbines provide clean energy by harnessing the wind.

I have also seen some solar farms, both nearby where I lived in Maryland as well as in Massachusetts, though they seem few and far between. I do recall one such farm which was built over a closed landfill. This seems like a good use of otherwise unusable land. However, an article in *The Week* indicated that there is a general disconnect between these sources of energy and the infrastructure that already exists so as to make best use of these alternative energy sources within the current power grid.[1]

While living in Massachusetts, I lived near a hydroelectric plant and I am aware of the energy that such plants produce, which is also a clean source of energy. Building such structures impacts communities in great ways, which is probably why they are not built often—their impact and their expense. Nonetheless, these three examples offer means of producing energy in clean ways, but they are limited in their scope to serve the needs of vast populations, unless such turbine or solar farms are expanded and efficiently incorporated into the present power grid. The only other known solution to the problem of a lack of energy sources seems to be nuclear

---

[1] The Week Staff, "Health and Science," *The Week*, Nov. 3, 2023, p. 21. https://usmagazine.theweek.com/full_page_image/the-week-us-2023-11-03-page-20/content.html.

power, which is always a thorny issue, given that everyone wants power and everyone wants it to be environmentally friendly, yet there are few working ideas about how to produce it—at least I am not aware of such.

Research into Alternative Sources of Energy

I am not a researcher, but it seems to me that there are very few alternatives to nuclear power currently on the horizon as viable sources for addressing our energy needs. Fossil fuels are polluting our environment at alarming levels, but we must assume that these reserves will be exhausted as energy needs from other countries also continue to expand. There can be no question that nuclear disasters have occurred throughout the world—Chernobyl (1986; Ukraine) and Fukushima Daiichi (2011; Japan) come to mind—but so does Three-Mile Island (1979; Pennsylvania). (I lived in Western Massachusetts in my youth, where the Yankee Atomic Plant provided energy to the region. It is no longer functioning.) Though these disasters are horrific to consider, nuclear power still appears to be a front-runner for present and future energy production, unless alternatives are found through research and development by academia, the private sector, and the government. France has used atomic power with great success, though I am told that their reactors are old and need updating.

Green Agenda

From my perspective, pushing a green agenda is laudable, but it needs to deal with the issue of energy production from the outset or it will never deal with the future of the United States or the world in an effective and lasting way, given that both China and India are poised to have hundreds of millions of people enter the middle class. Such development will force demands on sources of energy that have yet to be acknowledged on a global scale. In time, without innovation, this will be unsustainable. If such development is not scrutinized in a concerted way, we will see devastating disasters that the world has yet to experience over the issue of energy resources.

Recycling

I have made bold statements, not about global warming or other issues, which seem obvious, but about the production of energy. Since I believe that fossil fuels will run out, then alternative sources of energy are our only solution. We can, however, position ourselves in such a way that we maximize what we currently have in the best possible manner. Re-using what we have produced, as long as recycling requires less energy than making something from scratch, seems the best reworking of initial expenditures of energy.

As a youth growing up in Massachusetts, my family recycled metal cans as well as collected soda cans for redemption. There was a $.05 fee added to every soda can when purchased at stores. People received their money back when they redeemed the cans. We eventually collected various other materials as well: paper, magazines, plastics, and glass, which we would collect and put out with the trash in its own bin on the curb every two weeks. These would be picked up for a monthly fee, since this was not a service provided by our city. I have assisted others who collect similar materials and deliver them to a central site themselves. I believe in recycling and even the incentive for aluminum cans with the additional cost added at purchase, which can be recovered later. Such an effort can reduce littering. These simple steps, learned as children, can assist us in addressing the need to recycle at least part of the waste that we, as human beings, create as part of living. But these measures can and must be increased over time, otherwise the conspicuous consumption that we engage in will have devastating effects on everyone due to the actions of a few. No one can afford such wastefulness.

Environmental Matters

When it comes to environmental matters, a medial sense seems most objectively bound to achieve consensus. Mandating electric vehicles, for instance, without a sufficient number of charging stations or batteries capable of holding charges to conduct people lengthy distances needs to be evaluated against the ubiquity of gasoline cars and the facility with which they can be used and maintained. The expense of an electric car is currently beyond many people's reach. I have recently purchased a hybrid vehicle, which includes a battery, but the car runs primarily on gasoline. I have been reluctant to go all-in with an electric car because electric cars at my price point cannot cover the distances that I need to drive without sacrificing my time to lengthy recharging periods.

If we consider recycling, it makes sense in the long run, though my understanding of "single-stream" recycling points to the collectors taking care of sorting the items included for recycling. Computers could be recycled from one organization to another through amortization, but also through generosity. If a company upgrades and seeks to dispose of such assets, then partnering with a school or other non-profit may benefit all of the organizations. Managing data may need to be considered, but this is one suggestion for recycling.

When it comes to paper and glass and other items, someone needs to be able to break these materials down and make money in performing this operation. Energy needs should also be saved within this process, since less energy is used within this process than going from the original raw materials. Recycling is a good habit to develop, so that others can benefit from someone else's materials when that person has finished with them. "One person's junk is another person's treasure."

The point in general of saving energy and attempting to save the environment through clean methods of energy production is a great goal. But I'm not sure that the coal miners of West Virginia nor their members in Congress would agree. Their concern would be that if there is nothing to replace jobs lost within the coal and other industries, then there will be concern for the overall "cost" of total removal of coal from energy production, because cost can be understood in terms of jobs and opportunities. Coal and its disadvantages need to be weighed against its advantages in light of other methods of energy production that are available. But we need also to pursue other avenues for energy production, given that it seems that people's needs are growing, not diminishing, with regard to the consumption of energy.

Grains of Truth

Nonetheless, whatever issue people may espouse, grains of truth can often be found even within problematic positions. After all, addressing global warming due to an over-abundance of carbon dioxide in the atmosphere is a legitimate concern. How we go about diminishing pollutants must involve lowering emissions from cars, other vehicles, and factories; this is a given. The sense of how much we must lower emissions to realize progress is, however, a different story. People from one camp might suggest protracted measures, so that emission standards do not impact, for instance, the auto industry. Others may attempt to mandate electric cars through an established timeline, as policy makers have done in California, offering tax breaks for their purchase. Individuals on both sides are correct in their assessments, given that pollution is real and it is not going to get better on its own without mandates or other considerations, such as better gas mileage for cars, lightening cars' footprints, and a host of other concerns.

But what's involved in this and other discussions? I believe that it is an assessment of "winners" and "losers," which I think is an obsolete way of looking at such matters, rather than recognizing that impactful plans that are observed can deliver progress over time, where everyone both "loses" and "wins" in some fashion. Such an approach is typically called *consensus*, as long as the parties engaging in discussions are equally matched or otherwise have similar bargaining power to bring to the table.

For example, the autoworkers as a whole recently negotiated with management over the contracts that will bind them for several years. Negotiations meant that both sides needed to oversell their demands as they discussed benefits, wages, and the like. If only one worker were to negotiate his or her salary, that worker would be outmatched by management. Collective bargaining through a common spokesperson who speaks for all workers has a backing that management cannot ignore. Thus, negotiators are equally matched in this case, so the agreement, whatever it may be, will represent the best possible deal for all those involved. There's give and take on both sides. This is what is meant by losses and wins above.

If we return to a discussion of a position that involves "all-or-nothing" thinking, then people on one side disparage another's position or positions, because they might have to abandon something of worth to them in order to obtain a concession in another area. This type of logic follows from a sense of honor-shame, which is typically understood in all-or-nothing terms. From a sociological perspective, if I don't get everything that I want, then I have all of the shame from the given situation. If I do get everything that I want, then I have all of the honor. Such a perspective is played out throughout the Bible, but it's also found throughout the world in very different societies and cultures, though the same all or nothing thinking is at play. This is why groups kill others. The problem is that revenge subsequently perpetuates the problem with new players, so the honor-shame game continues without end.

Democracy, even though honor-shame values are sadly pervasive within its practice, especially through the use of political ads, is an attempt to preserve what I would call a more "civilized" sense of governance. Within democracy, people may not get everything that they want in relation to others, but *the Constitution* nonetheless ensures that there are appropriate separations that protect the various parties from each other, so that "the pursuit of happiness" is possible for everyone.

Compare and Contrast

In most areas of society, we make comparisons of some sort, but we have to establish norms and bases that provide us with foundational points. The easiest way of evaluating something is to compare and contrast it with something else. In doing this, however, there is typically bias involved within such evaluations. For instance, characters from literature are often portrayed in such a way that guides contrasts within the literary work, so that the author's intent is clear. If this does not occur, the meaning from the work might be indiscernible. But if there is no point to the writing, then why write or read it?

But when we come to political or other positions, it is important to maintain one's "distance" from what is being discussed, so that a person can come to an objective assessment of the facts. This is similar in scope to what a physician or judge would do in assessing evidence from scientific tests or the testimony of witnesses respectively. Objectivity, not emotion, should guide how people view what is presented, since the parties have vested interests in the outcome of the proceedings under evaluation. The more objective one can be, the fairer will such proceedings be. I tend toward believing that proceedings can reflect a level of fairness that can lead to further instances of equity. This is important.

Our society is rife with *professionals* who know how to push people's buttons. Lobbyists fulfill such a role. Political ads can demonize, that is, portray people in a negative light, as they can also brush over difficulties with positions as though they have no merit in assessing candidates' character or appropriateness for a political or other position. Both of these are extreme ways of handling political candidates—and they must be effective or members of all parties would not use them. But I wish to be clear that I cannot necessarily change this system of engagement. But I can control how I view these ads and the candidates portrayed within them, as well as how I will assess various issues, especially those that have to do with environmental and social concerns in relation to the agendas for and against wokeness, which is our prime matter for discussion.

The American People

When I use a term like "the American people," I believe it important to recognize the people one would include when considering such a term. In general, I believe that most people would recognize those who live in one's community first and foremost. The former Speaker of the House Thomas "Tip" O'Neil (D-Boston) once said that "all politics is local." We think about our communities first and we attempt to get what we can for them before anything else. I believe that this is a given.

The American Autoworkers (AAW) had their own concerns in play with their negotiations. But others, especially politicians, have to be concerned with their communities/constituencies, but also a broader spectrum of issues. For instance, if a member of Congress is able to "deliver" for his or her region, which means delivering federal funds for some sort of support for a local project, then that member may benefit from being voted in again. Promises that are delivered on can often translate into another term or terms in office. But what about the issues that have other circumstances in play that may not benefit a politician's constituency? This is where objectivity enters in.

In the long run, one must consider whether the measure being considered is something that will benefit a majority of people over time. Only a cost-benefit analysis can assess the efficacy of such measures. Voting for such measures can undermine one's chances of being voted in again, because many may be looking for some benefit at the individual or another level, whereas the elected official is looking at things from a wider view. This, too, can be a problematic, deliberative process because of its implications and impact. When we talk about the common good, do we mean the localized community or do we have something larger in view? This depends on the circumstance, as well as the person's view of that circumstance.

Human Resources

When we look at ad hoc situations, such as low water levels in the Colorado River or excessive urban sprawl or even excessive suburban development, then we should appreciate that we need problem-solving capabilities that look to the future to ensure that infrastructure holds and further expenditures are minimized. Yet, planners are also necessary to examine data that evaluates how the situation has developed to the point that exists. Some problems may seem obvious, such as Flint's lack of updates to repair their water pipes, which caused the problem with their drinking- water. This is fixable. But a lack of water in the Colorado River is not a fixable problem. Despite the drought, which has gone on for years, no one has addressed the broader point of water shortage to this and other desert regions, which has required an enormous amount of resources to "reclaim" it for the use of human beings. Changing the subject, in New Orleans, we saw that the Army Corps of Engineers successfully implemented a levy-system after Hurricane Katrina (2017), which held up in the wake of Hurricane Ida (2021). Unfortunately, the electrical system didn't fare as well. The telephone poles toppled under the pressure from the storm. Perhaps an underground system that utilizes protected, water-proof conduit through the already-established sewer system would be a better, more long-lasting response to implement. I don't know. I'm not an engineer.

But what America isn't doing currently, which it has in the past, is develop for the future, rather than for the moment, which means investing in our greatest resources: Americans themselves. By focusing so much on getting dollars into people's pockets for individual possession of resources, we have lost precious time and resources for investing in people with potential. The government does this—I know this for a fact. The National Institutes of Health (NIH) does this, as does the National Science

Foundation, through its charter. But do we as a people benefit from all of this or is the individual the only one to benefit?

Computers and Human Resources

I used the example of Amazon above not to pick on that company, but to illustrate a point through generally known data—at least as I have attempted to develop it. But something that all of the biggest companies are doing in order to gain profits is writing algorithms that track people's buying habits, thus attempting to make recommendations so that people will buy more. The problem with some of these algorithms is that some of them are habit-forming or addictive.

For myself, I noted that, in using YouTube, the site would identify what videos I most watched and then recommend others that were similar. I found that I was devoting a great deal of time to these videos when I viewed them—with no end of recommendations ever reached. But then I read somewhere about settings that I could alter, so that the program would not make these recommendations. I searched high and low for these settings, but I found that I had to scroll down the screen in a deliberate fashion in order to find and alter the setting. This was suspicious to me, until I read that some game-makers deliberately make their games addictive. I also watched *60 Minutes* and found that officials at various companies, like Google, did not permit their own children to use their smartphones for more than an hour each day. They admitted that there are addictive components within the programs that they are delivering for the consumption of the general public. This needs to change.

Responsibility—Again

I use a computer for hours each day and I believe that I am a savvy computer user. But when I go to the Amazon web-site, I am inundated with attempts to sell me various items. Whenever I click, another screen pops up. It drives me crazy, but I still complete my order and obtain what I want. But I have used streaming subscriptions through Amazon: Amazon Prime Video, Paramount+, and others. There are many recommendations on my television screen when I select them, but I have to admit that I don't know how to stop some of these recommendations, so I don't bother doing so. I suppose that I could call someone at Amazon and that person would help me, which I have done with great success in the past, but my motto is: *If it's not obvious what I should do, then it needs to change*. It is incumbent upon Amazon or any other company to ensure that their services function according to expectations, so that I get what I want. But I should also be able to eliminate what I *don't* want easily. This is basic customer service. Otherwise, I believe that I am being manipulated. This is something else that needs to change.

These comments may be far afield from green concerns, but I believe that being green also has to do with operating in a fashion that is responsible. If this is not the case, then everyone loses, except Amazon. This is the type of situation that needs to be rectified, so that consumers and providers are operating on a level playing field. I am not against how our economy operates. What I am against is a giant company like Amazon or Google or Facebook standing aloof from their responsibility *not* to use algorithms that addict people into buying things or using their services in a manner that they do not need or otherwise remaining on their web-sites for excessive lengths of time, when they wouldn't permit their own children to do this. This is not responsible; this is highly problematic behavior.

Conclusion

Being green means attempting to use resources in a responsible manner, not only for the time being, but also for the future. If someone uses a tree, then one ought to be planted in its place. There are zones in the US that need to be preserved from any sort of harm, oil drilling, fracking, and the like. Our national parks should be maintained as pristinely as possible. But we also need to recognize that our present energy requirements are not being served solely by renewable sources. In fact, renewable sources have not been effectively incorporated into the US power grid. This needs to change, but our country as a whole, in union with others, needs to develop clean energy sources for the future. I do not know of anyone who believes that energy consumption will decrease. Instead, the problem of developing energy alternatives must continue to be supported in earnest through industry, the government, and through international initiatives for the benefit of those who contribute. Unless this takes place, we will not be preparing for the future in a concerted way, but will instead be bypassing this important need. This represents a misguided path. Instead, by smart investing in green energy sources apart from those already developed, both the US and the world can work in a green direction. This, it seems to me, will foster realizing a better future for all of us.

In the next chapter, we will explore what it means to be "woke," given that I personally was ignorant of what this term implied, yet it is bantered about frequently by politicians and others.

3 AWAKE, NOT WOKE

The term, "woke," first used in an African American song dealing with racial injustice, has to do at its root with a general concern over racial and other injustices within our society.[2] There is a consistent banter in political circles and in society at large around woke culture, oftentimes described in negative terms. It can be difficult to find positive aspects of something that someone does not like—or even hates—but it is, nonetheless, important to do so, otherwise we will lack objectivity, which can slant any fair evaluation or assessment. A bumper sticker that I once saw encapsulates my own sentiment: "I'm awake, but not woke." In other words, there are aspects of woke concerns that are compelling, whereas there are those that are not. I believe that this is true for any position, given that the good and the bad often cohere where human beings are involved, though who is to say what is "good" and what is "bad"? This, too, can be a matter for discussion, but I believe that considering racial injustice can help to appreciate what is at stake from several perspectives.

Systemic and Other "-Ism's"

For proofs in mathematics, it is difficult to develop an all-encompassing theory for how numbers function. Some devote their entire lives to solving

[2] Domenico Montenaro, "What Does the Word 'Woke' Really Mean, and Where Does It Come From?" *National Public Radio* (NPR), July 19, 2023. https://www.npr.org/2023/07/19/1188543449/what-does-the-word-woke-really-mean-and-where-does-it-come-from.

one complex problem, which means that the solution is elusive or otherwise evades mathematicians due to all of the possibilities that such a problem can involve. However, one need only produce one counter argument or exception to demonstrate that the theory or hypothetical solution is incorrect or implausible. In sum, this means that it is easier to disprove something than to prove it.

It is stemming from just such an understanding that we must examine the issue or problem of various "-isms," such as racism or sexism or ageism. Many people attempt to associate such a term, for instance, with typically poor treatment that they have received, when, in fact, people cannot and should not necessarily jump to a universal conclusion before they have attempted to discount other possibilities for these poor experiences. It is difficult to draw conclusions from only a few experiences of some occurrence. Extrapolating outside of the simplest solution seems prevalent in society. Instead, we ought to appreciate whether situations do, in fact, reflect the simplest solutions, or do they instead reflect something much broader? This is not an easy assessment to make, yet it seems appropriate, given the seemingly widespread nature of how people are associating one "-ism" or another as the reason behind other people's actions. Our nation is founded upon laws, which are further based on people's presumption of innocence. This ought to be our standard, unless the proof points us in another direction.

"-Isms"

Racism, sexism, and ageism, as three representative cases among others, are terms that appreciate a systematic discrimination or hatred against people of a specific race, gender, or age group, which typically end in some sort of negative consequences. All of these terms represent collectives or groupings of people who receive the onus of other people's hatred or poor treatment simply because they belong to one of these targeted groups. In other words, people are viewed as members of one of these groups over and above their bearing as individuals. Thus, the collective identity is what is evaluated, not the individual's personal identity.

I'm not sure that seeing people within a collective identity is necessarily problematic. Scientific understandings can identify certain groups of people who have a propensity toward certain diseases. Tay sachs disease is associated with Ashkenazi (European) Jews. Sickle-cell anemia is associated primarily with African Americans. There are genes that implicate certain women as having a higher propensity toward breast cancer. All of these factors, as determined through scientific research, have demonstrated that certain genetic predispositions can lead in these directions. Science is not biased, but instead is based on evidence that supports its claims, not to cast aspersions on any group of people, but to note genetic mutations that may lead toward appreciating specific conditions. This information helps to develop cures for these conditions. Thus, isolating these genes can have a positive or neutral purpose.

Negative Implications

When, however, someone uses the term "racism" or "sexism" or "ageism," it typically means that there is some negative consequence that was experienced due to the presence of some form of patterned or systematic behavior, where actions were not simply negative outcomes of situations, such as someone having a bad day or some other rational explanation for the negative events at hand. Nonetheless, one must, as in a scientific or forensic manner, determine whether some negative experience stems from an overt behavior or is otherwise problematic due to the presence of one these "-ism"'s. Such a position should, however, not be assumed. People must demonstrate repeatable facts in order to prove that the outcome is a manifestation of discrimination. If facts do not correlate with such a conclusion, then the event or events may have been part of a negative experience, but whether they reflect an -ism must still be proven.

Passive Racism

One isolated case does not constitute racism or sexism or ageism. I can recall a bookkeeper speaking to a group of people and using the expression, "Jew him down," meaning to argue with someone about getting a better deal. I was shocked by the expression and brought it to the chair of the board, who was absent at the time the statement was made, but who was also Jewish. He said that he was going to deal with it in his own way. This person was the woman's boss, but he did not find that the woman's conduct was bigoted toward him. He told me that this expression, as heinous as it may have been, was something that he had heard before, but it was something that he did not believe was the woman's fault. I called the remark prejudiced, but, from my understanding, it was passive, not active prejudice. The woman had not chosen this expression to hurt this individual. It was one that she knew and used without thinking.

I know others who, in common parlance, may use racial epithets in their conversations, again, without necessarily thinking about the nature of the terms that they use. I know for a fact that these individuals have close friends who are members of the races identified by such expressions. Again, I would suggest that such expressions are passive in nature and character. It does not preclude the possibility for correction, so that a different pattern of behavior can be evinced, but such behaviors should not be associated with "being" racist or sexist or ageist per se. They are learned behaviors that are problematic, but I do not believe that they are overtly troublesome nor do they undermine society. All or nothing thinking is by its nature authoritarian. I express my reservations about appreciating such behaviors as innately prejudiced, because they are not deliberate. One's intentionality matters.

Systemic Racism

There are some instances of conduct that reasonable people would associate with actually being racist. Negatively targeting another race through violence is obvious. Police forces that have targeted African Americans are described as engaging in racist behaviors only after investigators determine through police reports and other data that such targeting has taken place, which has recently been shown to be the case in various areas around the country. But to say that police forces in general are racist is a highly controversial, inflammatory and problematic statement. There must be proof to demonstrate such a contention.

Sensitivity Training

Sensitivity training has its place within the grand scheme of society, but there also has to be an appreciation for how some groups, due to their collective and other identity, view different people. It is an imposed understanding that everyone ought to be who he or she believes oneself to be. For those who come from collective identities, the sense of belonging to one's group is of paramount importance, not one's so-called personal identity. American culture tends to emphasize the individual, but cultural awareness appreciates that people of different races oftentimes do not appreciate such a sense to the extent that others do. People from most of Asia, Central and South America, Native Americans, Africa, and other regions, generally understand the group to be more important than the individual, and people will see themselves within such a cultural identity over an individual one. Sensitivity training can oftentimes set up models of identity that may not have a foundation in fact or recognize the collective understandings of different people.

A friend recently pointed out that training on racism and other similar concerns was "encouraged" for teachers, where teachers needed to learn how their "status" being "White" gave them a sense of entitlement that would preclude their ability to see other people as being "oppressed." This is an example of a false narrative. The collective sense of being White is being used as a tool to form a collective for all people who are White. On the other side of this controversy, people see themselves as oppressed, presumably at the hands of those who are privileged. This is far from accurate. It is not necessarily based in fact.

I come from a poor family, which happens to be White. Do I have more in common with White people who are middle to upper middle class or above, or with poor Blacks or Asians? The economic factor thus enters into the picture, given that it can implicate a person's relative success in life, as can other aspects besides race, gender, or something else. In other words, it is important to recognize factual aspects rather than conjecture about how people have attained their place in society relative to others. Race is one factor among several others. Negative treatment may have occurred due to another's negative perspective toward someone's race; however, such a perspective should not be assumed. Again, assessment of the facts is needed to discern whether racism in fact played a role in the situation under consideration. Just because people yell "racism" or "sexism" or "ageism" does not mean that these issues played a role in how some circumstances have played themselves out.

Narrative

People's narratives or stories of their lives unfold over time. They rely upon many different factors to bring this about. If someone has experienced some form of abuse or racism or another -ism at others' hands, then this can impact how people's lives progress. I cannot argue with such an assertion, as long as it stems from facts.

But there are also people who have overcome seemingly impossible odds to advance in society and elsewhere. I am not citing such individuals to discount ill-treatment, which ought to be remedied, but in general, every collective appreciates individuals who can overcome odds tilted against them. They can overcome negative odds and make their situations other than the typical trajectory than they are on. Nonetheless, those who own their narratives and do with them what they can, despite tragedy and difficulty, are people whom most people can celebrate and admire. This is a great achievement. It does not address the ill treatment of those who have actually been kept down through systematic or other racism or sexism or ageism, but it does underscore how people can overcome what seem like insurmountable forces or odds in order to advance in unparalleled ways.

Racism and People of Color

A family member shared with me that the deed to his house had a statement in it that excepted purchase of it by people of color. This is flagrant racism, and such measures need to be eradicated from our society. We have recently heard of instances that have demonstrated innate bias against Blacks within the military and elsewhere, such as in Oklahoma, one hundred years ago, and other more recent events, at least drawing from such events portrayed on the evening news. I do not doubt the presence of racism and associated practices in some places in our country. Nonetheless, without substantive proof of its presence through systematic actions and practices, I am hard-pressed to recognize how broad this problem is. Where it is provable, then those who are responsible must be held accountable and appropriately punished, as has been proven in police departments in various locales throughout the country. However, I do not presume racist tendencies unless evidence demonstrates otherwise.

The Supreme Court has struck down affirmative action initiatives for colleges, which attempt to offset the damage caused by preferential practices that some of the finest colleges and universities have used for admissions. I must admit that, though my father attended Williams College in Western Massachusetts, for only a year or two—he graduated from Bryant College, which was then in Providence, Rhode Island—I was nonetheless considered a *legacy*, and my application was favored. I cannot say by how much or in what way this occurred—only that it was taken into account. We might view my case as preferential treatment, but I would be hesitant to call it "White privilege." The fact is that, prior to 1970, I believe, Williams College was an all-male college. Additionally, given this fact, it was a good assumption that, if someone's father gave money after graduation to an institution, then it was more likely that a family member would do the same to that school (legacy). I'm not sure that I would call this scenario favoritism due to race as much as a good business model. Be this as it may, this is another issue that one can appreciate from multiple angles. There isn't one conclusion to draw from the data presented above. This is why multiple points of view must be held in contrast and tension to appreciate what *a* (not *the*) truth about the matter might involve.

I am certain that there are locations where racism is operative. However, I am hard-pressed to draw from such a notion that racism is a problem everywhere in the country. I admit to my own limited experience with this issue, so my discussion of racism must also be limited.

Cultural Changes

Significant cultural changes have already occurred with the generational transitions that have taken place in our country, where the Silent Generation (1928-1945) that participated in World War II is virtually gone, and other generations: Baby Boomers (1946-1964), Gen X (1965-1980), Millennials or Gen Y (1981-2000), Generation Z or iGen or Centennials (2001 to 2020), then Gen Alpha (2010's-2025), have come or are coming on the scene.[3] We have seen recently how some members of

---

[3] Michele Debczak, "These Revised Guidelines Redefine Birth Years and Classifications for Millennials, Gen Z, and Gen Alpha," *Mental Floss*, Dec. 6, 2019; updated Mar. 10,

Congress have held on to their seats of power into their eighties and even nineties. This is remarkable, but it also demonstrates how slowly Congress changes. This can be a good thing, but must be weighed with objectivity as we presented above. Do we need to consider term or age limits?

The movements that emerged during Covid, such as Black Lives Matter, seemed to focus on accountability. Incidents occurred that incited many people to promote such concerns. Yet, with any movement, my concern is not with the "philosophy" of the group's proposals, but with how people live out their understanding of how things ought to come together. Accountability has been demanded of the police and other groups—and rightfully so. But when push comes to shove, many groups who advocate such accountability on the part of others do not manifest it within their own lives or actions.

Maturity

From my own studies in education, people tend not to take ownership of their actions until late adolescence or later, and even then, there is still a learning period, which involves trial and error. Taking ownership of one's actions is what maturity means to me. Only when people can assess their own behavior and act from a sense of objectivity in relation to it, even to the point of evaluating their own actions as negative, can a person be understood to be mature. When, instead, our self-interests overpower a sense of ethics or morals, then people cannot claim to be pressing for appropriate change, because change must always begin with me. I can point the finger of judgment at others, but if I cannot assess the legitimacy of my own actions first, then I have no business looking at others, when I cannot deal with what is going on inside me or the consequences of my own actions. Movements that develop from such a mature center can propel society toward positive, productive change. But this does not occur as much when issues are "heart-felt," except when they reflect the inner disposition and actions of those living out of such changes within their own lives. Our country is full of issues and concerns. Those that gain

---

2023. https://www.mentalfloss.com/article/609811/age-ranges-millennials-and-generation-z. Some figures have been altered from the original source. The source has been cited to reveal the various naming conventions associated with the generations.

traction can do so through both adolescent or mature means. The question seems to be whether consensus is possible, which is based in and on trust, or if people are attempting to "strong-arm" others into capitulation, because honor-shame concerns are operative. Only objective assessment can determine which type of perspective a person or group is attempting to bring to bear on the problem or issue.

Conclusion

Our discussion of wokeness did not deal explicitly with this position, because every position has positive and negative aspects that ought to be considered. The discussion did, however, recognize that there is always a reason to pause before acting, especially deliberating about what is important: What will be lost and what will be gained, and who will be affected. The suggestion that full-blown change will only deliver good to the nation or some group lacks such objectivity. This is a naïve stance. Instead, a medial approach to change seems better suited to accommodate legitimate concerns from the various sides of any discussion. Of course, people can stall and undermine progress. These are the actions of the immature who wish to maintain things the way that they currently are, which typically means that they also benefit from the situation as it is. If society as a whole continues to tolerate such immature posturing, then government inaction, as we have seen in Congress, will continue to undermine progress in the nation. Immaturity, not maturity, will continue to flourish and win the day.

The problems facing our nation are too complex and enormous to continue along the same path that we have been traveling. Consensus, not all or nothing thinking, is one way to bring various parties to the table to discuss the intricacies of such problems. They may develop from different perspectives, but such perspectives can bring depth to discussions. Without another approach, the American people will continue to pay their taxes, but the benefits of doing so will dwindle.

The next chapter will discuss flexibility and security and how these aspects interact to formulate a possible way forward.

4 FLEXIBILITY AND SECURITY

I once had a meeting with a future boss, who repeatedly asked me whether I could attend meetings on the one day off that I would have per week. I stated that there was plenty of time before I came on board to change the day of standard meetings or even for me to change my day off if need be. This appeared not to be an option. Instead, the person wanted me sometimes to lose the evening of my day off, though another person in the meeting, seemingly the voice of reason, indicated how important a consistent day off is for a person. I agreed. In sharing this episode with yet another person, she identified that the encounter sounded like concerns over flexibility and security. I was emphasizing security, namely, a "secure" day off during the week that I could call my own, when I could do what *I* wanted to do, which is what a day off from work is supposed to be. The other person was testing the waters for how flexible I was. This seems like a valid appreciation for how people interact on a general basis. One or more individuals or groups highlight security over against those who emphasize flexibility. I believe that using such a model as a foundation for an inquiry into various issues in society and other arenas is pertinent toward revealing how we currently find ourselves in American culture.

The Chronicles of Riddick

The Chronicles of Riddick (2004) is a sci-fi movie directed by David

Twohy, starring Vin Diesel as Riddick.[4] The film is set in the future, where space-travel is commonplace. Riddick is a Furian warrior, that is, he comes from this race of people. He is being pursued by bounty hunters, though he always bests them. In this film, which is one of a series, he is also pursued by an intergalactic group known as the Necromongers. These individuals take on world after world with their armada of ships and soldiers, decimating the population, then destroying the planets themselves. Before doing so, they take the citizenry captive and put them through a process of "purification," whereby they adopt the Necromonger ideology through a painful process, which helps them to appreciate one pain overcoming another. Their leader is the Lord Marshall, who has been to the holy place of all Necromongers, "the Underverse." His experience has changed him. He is faster, stronger, and more agile than anyone else, so he invites combat against those who do not wish to abandon their faiths to convert to that of the Necromongers, which he always wins.

On one world, where Riddick witnesses the invitation to conversion of the now conquered people, one of the leaders stands up to the Lord Marshall, only to have what seems to be his soul removed from his body by the Lord Marshall, which is witnessed by all of the people in attendance. The sight causes them to drop to their knees in obeisance before him. For his part, Riddick is taken into custody, where he is examined by supernatural forces, but he evades capture. The Lord Marshall fears Riddick, given his Furian heritage, due to an earlier prophecy which describes his overthrow by a Furian.

At the end of the film, Riddick squares off against the Lord Marshall, but he is no match for him. Yet, when he tries to take Riddick's soul, Riddick "holds on" to it in a manner never before witnessed, which baffles the Lord Marshall and everyone else present. In light of this apparent weakness on the Lord Marshall's part, Riddick's position is assisted through a mutiny within the ranks of the Necromongers, which facilitates Riddick's killing of the Lord Marshall. The Necromongers' motto is: "Take what you kill," meaning that the spoils go to the victor, so Riddick becomes the new leader

---

[4] *The Chronicles of Riddick*. Directed by David Twohy. Universal Pictures. 2004. https://en.wikipedia.org/wiki/The_Chronicles_of_Riddick_(franchise). Last ed. 7 March 2024.

of the Necromongers, as they all kneel before him. This is where the movie ends.

Sense of Identity

Riddick is flexible in his ability to face challenges and challengers, eventually besting all of them. This is due to a particularly dense sense of self. Many attempt to imprison him or otherwise kill him, but he always comes out on top. He eventually even becomes the Lord Marshall, as strange an outcome as ever could be.

Yet Riddick's character confronts the Necromongers, who are looking to destroy huge populations by their efforts to "convert" others to their faith, which is based on the outlook of their strongest warrior, the Lord Marshall. We might look at the Necromongers as representative of many groups that attempt to gain adherents to their cause. Those who are strong from other groups are killed, whereas those who witness such killings must acquiesce or meet a similar fate. We can appreciate that most people fit into the "in-between" realm of those who have different levels of belief. Those who are as strong as Riddick can receive great honor, yet Riddick is Furian. He is a particular type of humanoid, who can handle himself in virtually any circumstance, whose mettle has been tested over and over again.[5]

Who's In? Who's Out?

Within any group, there is usually some form of indicator that identifies that a person is in or out. Many groups use uniforms to identify their members, where, as in the police, fire department, and military, there are insignias that identify rank and position within an otherwise indiscernible grouping of people. The identifiable "white coat" or stethoscope in a hospital often points to a physician or sometimes a nurse. The black robe in a courtroom usually indicates the presiding judge. Mechanics often wear a grey or blue shirt with their name sewn into it. Some in industry wear lanyards with badges that show their picture and name. Whatever is used

[5] I do not deny that I may be reading more into *the Chronicles of Riddick* than is warranted, yet it can still serve as a metaphor for appreciating what is at stake within the understanding of flexibility and security that we are discussing.

to identify membership within a particular grouping of people, this serves to demonstrate who is in, but also serves to identify who is out, so that "security" can monitor and control entry points for a host of reasons.

For instance, if customers come to a work site, then they need to be granted entry, otherwise the business will fail. If hostile entities appear, then civil authorities may need to be summoned to handle such a threat. In other words, groups maintain who is in the group to ensure the group's identity and integrity, but those who wish to gain admittance must be evaluated in some way. After all, if someone was just hired by a company, then this person needs to be granted access despite having no badge, so there must be a protocol for entry in such a case. In other words, we could characterize access to groups as a dance that takes place between flexibility and security in maintaining boundaries of access, where there must be sufficient flexibility to permit new members to join the group, but there must also be enough security to guard the boundary as well. How much of each is necessary is dependent on those who watch these borders, but what happens in the extreme?

Passport Control

I have travelled abroad many times and I have always been impressed by the customs agents who take passports from people arriving from all over the world to enter their country. In just a few seconds, the agents have to assess the information provided from the passport on a computer screen as well as the person providing the passport, oftentimes dealing with someone who is tired due to jet lag. The greeting that they exchange and the response to the question: "What are you doing in *this country*?" are all that the customs official has to go on. The agent has to assess if the people are being truthful in their assertions, which may be difficult to ascertain. Nonetheless, these agents must deal with a huge number of people during their shift and they can only rely on instinct to recognize when someone poses a threat, the passport itself notwithstanding, given that certain individuals or countries of origin may be flagged for some reason. This is an enormous responsibility on the part of these individuals, yet it seems similar in scope to the mail sorter that I've seen on television that directs mail depending on the first three digits in the zip code. It is an enormously difficult task, yet trained people perform such duties daily. I am sure that in the future some type of artificial intelligence (AI) will be used to enhance this process. I have seen how face recognition is used in some countries in various ways. Nonetheless, for the time being, a human assessment in literally seconds is what permits people to pass through airports or other border control facilities to enter other countries.

Reasons for Visiting

Reasons for visiting another country vary greatly, depending on the person involved. Some may be going on vacation or for another stay of short duration. Others may be beginning or continuing the process of setting up residence in a given country. Some may be going to conduct business. Once again, there is no “one-size-fits-all” understanding for why people visit other countries, though other reasons may be due to insecurity in one’s country of origin, which could involve concern over one’s physical safety or due to economic hardship or something else. Whatever the reason, however, it is varied. Looking at the reasons behind why people come to the US will deliver a plethora of answers as well.[6]

Considering Integrity

Flexibility and security, then, presume that there is a set of values that cohere to give a group identity and integrity. I would suggest that the less security there is within the integrity of the group, the more security will be demanded at its borders, understood both figuratively and literally. Oftentimes, groups will focus on external security, obfuscating a lack of inner cohesion. If there is insufficient integrity within the group related to its identity, then the group in question will disintegrate due to a lack of inner cohesion revolving around a specific set of values. Additionally, if there is an insufficient number of members, then the group will lose its integrity due to a lack of members over time. Both internal cohesion or integrity of values plus a critical mass of contributing members must come together to maintain any group. There must also be a core group of “true believers,” who can serve as the “heart” of the group. In general, group dynamics describe how 15-20% of group members maintain the group’s

---

[6] We will examine the issue of so many migrants at the southern border below in chapter 7.

integrity.

Attracting Members

Additionally, there must be an effort to attract new members to the group or the group will become unhealthy, dysfunctional, or simply die out. In order to obtain new members, some "marketing" techniques must be used to connect with a different audience. If the current group is stagnant in growth from its current audience and the pool of applicants from it, then this often means that this resource has been exhausted or that the message of the group has become stale or is otherwise no longer attractive for a host of reasons. We have to appreciate that a different approach is in order. This might involve security and flexibility, and how much "tolerance" is possible in maintaining the integrity of the core of the group, but also how much flexibility a group is willing to accept or even endure in order to move forward to enhance its membership rolls. If too much flexibility is permitted, then the core values will suffer. If too little flexibility is granted, then the group's membership will remain stagnant or even decrease. However, being welcoming, open, and honest about a group are attitudes that should never be overlooked; they should be a constant, since they transcend any other group values. In general, people want to be a part of an inviting group, whereas they will run from a suspicious one. A group should put its best foot forward in seeking out new members to join. Such an effort should never become routinized or "old hat." These are off-putting attitudes. Invitations to join the core of the group bolsters the integrity of the group, but not everyone can maintain such a commitment nor should such an invitation be granted too quickly. Such an invitation should only come after someone has demonstrated willingness to help the group to grow and develop, especially by manifesting the group's core values.

Leaders of Groups

It is often difficult to characterize what qualities reflect ideal leaders of groups, since this will often depend on the group in question. I would suggest that first and foremost must be a concern for the individual members, both the people already in the group and those who are seeking membership, as well as the core values themselves. In other words, empathy for other people's concerns needs to be found in leaders. When a leader recognizes the needs of new members, then this can help a leader to determine whether a person is a good fit for the group. Such a concern for other people underscores the integrity of the group. It is one thing to phrase such a matter in terms of the member's needs, which means that the leader has listened to the other person and determined that there is no fit. It is yet another to be off-putting to such an extent that it devalues another person. Groups in the past often used a methodology of "us and them" to entice people to join. I believe that such a method would now work against them.

Another quality of an ideal leader is the ability on important occasions to share why he or she is a member of the particular group, but especially when soliciting for new members. Personal testimony can serve as an opportunity for someone with an unvoiced question to appreciate what the group can do for him or her. I cannot say that I have heard such testimony often, yet, when I have, it has served as a poignant reminder to me and to others. The speaker engendered respect for the sharing, but also appreciation of what the group had to offer. These are powerful draws for joining a group, but they also betoken reasons for not joining. Thus, when people do not join, it is not necessarily the case that the group is "broken" in some way, but that it does not suit the needs of the people seeking membership.

In general, excellent interpersonal skills are often touted as something needed in leaders, and I believe that this is true to some extent. However, when people demonstrate through actions how they live out the values of the group, yet may have some deficiencies with interpersonal skills, such matters can be overlooked, because there are other internal values that are recognized by on-lookers. We should appreciate that externals matter, such as appropriate decorum and the like, but groups become healthy and functional when internal resources take hold, where the externals no longer matter that much. Externals are needed initially, but people's interior understanding of the group's purpose should deepen over time. If things remain superficial, which I have seen more often than not, then people's connection to the group will not deepen and they will not adopt the core values. Such a group will eventually die out or become irrelevant.

Mission of the Group

A mission statement for a group is important, but the statement is merely a summary of other deeper values that the group has. However, if there is no clear understanding or articulation of the group's mission, then the group's values will be ambiguous and so will be the connections among the members. I have seen groups that boast great numbers of members, yet I have also witnessed members' inability to state the simplest of the group's values. This is not good for the group's future, since the group in question had no opportunities for deepening group development that I saw. There may be many members, but their depth and identity as group members were lacking. Such a group will eventually die out.

There is as well another dimension to mission, namely, through outreach opportunities of various sorts. Many groups focus on helping others, which is a wonderful thing. Many people will sign up to perform various acts of charity, such as providing food for those in need; partnering with Habitat for Humanity or other similar outreach activities. But the question remains whether a person is willing to embrace the core values of the organization more or less over time. Activities can often serve to focus people's time, energy, and attention on external matters, which is good in itself. But can a group move at least a part of people's attention toward the group's values without alienating members whose attention is more dissipated? Social groups have their value, but there are no core values that help to align people with one another within these groups, which means that, over time, when the social aspects fall away, what is left? Social interactions serve as a means to foster concerns over core values, but such interactions should never be seen as exclusive to the social scene. The social should be subject to promoting core values, not the other way around. The reverse is a death-knell for any group, since the social will dominate.

Gradual Commitment

"Moving up the ranks" within the police force, military, or other similar groups is clear. Promotion happens through identifiable means and stages. The most successful groups that I know of are clear about requirements for promotion and how to achieve it. Such promotions are external representations of what may or may not be happening at an interior level, but the rank is at least something to consider if only as an external indicator. Boy Scouts and Girl Scouts and their members working toward merit badges come to mind, so that children, growing in their commitment to the core values of these organizations, have a steady, gradual approach to achieving something, as they spend their time working toward identifiable goals. I have seen some churches attempt to follow such a methodology to their benefit and success, whereas others have not and they are losing members. Clarity is key. When the objectives are obfuscated or commandeered to advance values that do not represent the core values of the organization, then there will be problems to face, but, over time, such diversions should serve to help a group to re-focus, re-group, and re-establish its core values, not go in a different direction.

Sexual Abuse

The Catholic Church's core values never espoused sexual abuse of any sort, but such things did take place. Given the world-wide scope of this organization, the crisis has crippled people's understanding of the Church's core values wherever allegations have surfaced, because they have obfuscated its assistance of the poor and other vulnerable populations. Yet sex abuse has also affected the Boy Scouts, as well as colleges and universities, other churches and synagogues, hampering their humanitarian efforts due to the crisis. The military, too, has had to rise to meet its responsibilities in addressing allegations. All areas of society, including business, have had to stop and examine their part to play in turning a blind eye to sexual abuse at various levels of leadership and various levels of commitment. Most of these institutions have enacted responses that protect others from sexual predation. This must become a part of core values for the integrity of these organizations. This underscores a group's ability to adapt, which is a modern value, but a good one.

Core Values and Forgiveness

Leaders of the organizations listed above have addressed the sex abuse crisis in various ways. Once again, flexibility in conducting oneself within one of these organizations is weighed against the security necessary to ensure that no predation or grooming behaviors can take place, which can lead to further problems. But this is another quality of a true leader. He or she is willing to accept that not everything that an organization has done is perfect, including one's own conduct. Egregious behaviors are hard to reconcile, whereas humility in light of one's personal darkness is something that has the potential for forgiveness, a religious core value. We have become a nation that lacks forgiveness: We have forgotten our connection with our founders' religious roots. One's core values should be in evidence both toward one's own group as well as toward others if they are truly core values. This is the nature of due process, at least as I see it.

Core Values and Lifestyles

Yet I also recognize that some lifestyle choices have entered the mainstream, whereas others have not. Homosexual marriage is the law of the land. People need not embrace this lifestyle or otherwise support it, but it is the law, and the law needs to be respected and observed. However, issues surrounding transgenderism have attempted to ally themselves with issues related to sexual orientation. This does not necessarily follow.

Our discussion is primarily related to how security and flexibility dance with each other in maintaining their understandings. Transgenderism is a minority view within a minority view. The position that gender is a "construct" is not based in or on science, according to an *OpEd* in *The Wall Street Journal*, which I found compelling, written in tandem by an evolutionary biologist and developmental biologist.[7] Sexual orientation may be influenced by societal norms or genetics, this is true, but the vast majority of people across the globe are not gender dysphoric, which develops naturally, but need not be acted upon.

There are cases where children are biologically ambiguous in relation to their gender at birth; this is also true. Parents make a choice in consultation with their physicians about what to do in such a case. However, the present current of discussion is that gender dysphoria needs to be fostered or

---

[7] Colin M. Wright and Emma N. Hilton, "The Dangerous Denial of Sex," *The Wall Street Journal*, 14 Feb 2020. https://www.wsj.com/articles/the-dangerous-denial-of-sex-11581638089. Mr. Wright is an evolutionary biologist at Penn State. Ms. Hilton is a developmental biologist at the University of Manchester.

otherwise acted upon immediately, especially within psycho-therapeutic environments. This seems like a problematic strategy, given the implications of sex-reassignment surgery and other hormone-based treatments. If, over time, working with therapists and physicians, someone elects to have gender-reassignment surgery after their period of puberty, then this is their prerogative in conscience. Normative practices of society are not necessarily detrimental to the individual just because they represent the majority sense of how society currently operates. For instance, from the presentation above, the practice of forcing others to use one's "preferred" pronouns could undermine the group in which such a person attempts to function. This is not discrimination per se, since a person has chosen one's gender. It is not similar in scope to one's ethnic origin, religious affiliation, or sexual orientation, which are not chosen in the same manner as one's gender can be. It is confusing and can cause division, not cohesion for a group.

There is rhetoric denouncing which bathrooms transgender individuals should use. A solution for such an impasse is to move toward unisex, single bathrooms, which can be used by everyone. I have been in municipalities where certain guidelines are mandated, such as parking facilities located beneath new construction in Washington, DC. Why not have all new buildings include unisex bathrooms in future construction? The point then becomes moot at least in this case. It worked in relation to the Americans with Disabilities Act. Why not follow a similar model? In other words, such a strategy avoids the problem by also avoiding unnecessary drama.

Hostility Toward Groups

There are always seemingly two or more opinions about anything in our country, where people's sensibilities weigh in more or less depending on how much a given issue affects such groups. I would suggest, however, that the model of punishing another group when it does not conform to one's sense of how things should proceed should be avoided at all cost. One need only consider the hostility against some religious and other groups that has surfaced in our country.

There will always be divergences between groups; this is a given. But a case like the one that went before the Supreme Court between an Amish community and a municipality comes to mind. The municipality in Minnesota established guidelines for bringing something about that involved farming. The guidelines did not reflect how the Amish operated their farms, so the municipality took Amish land by eminent domain for failure to comply with these policies. The Supreme Court found in favor of the Amish with the following summary: "In this country, neither the Amish nor anyone else should have to choose between their farms and their faith."[8]

Religious faith should not subject people to societal or other prejudice, yet this does happen, even by governmental entities. The separation of Church and State is a sound premise, but maintaining it requires walking a fine line among values like compliance, tolerance, faithfulness to one's conscience, exceptions, and the like, though once again, we are considering flexibility and security. The municipality attempted to secure its guidelines while trampling on the religious freedom of the Amish. The Supreme Court sadly had to weigh in, because there was no one at the grass roots willing to consider both sides fairly. The precedent is now established. From another perspective, I am aware that there are Chaplains in the military who are designated as "limited," where, for instance, a Catholic Chaplain would not perform a wedding for a homosexual couple, though one participant was a member of the military. Catholic Chaplains also hear confessions for Catholics, though most Chaplains could offer counseling to all military members, no matter one's denomination. There are distinctions that need to be maintained within and outside military service, so that the separation of Church and State is consistent across the board.

Hostility from Other Quarters

The violence, even murder, perpetrated against church-members or synagogue-members is a growing trend in our country. We can identify the perpetrators' problem as stemming from "mental illness," but I don't believe that this is the whole issue, nor do I believe that such a stance

---

[8] U. S. Supreme Court, *Mast vs. Fillmore County*, July 2, 2021.

contributes substantively to the issue.[9] Instead, I would suggest that there are (primarily) (young) men who have become disenfranchised in our country, who are willing to engage in violence against others to assuage their inability to connect with significant others, especially other males. They instead use violence to express their rage, an outward expression, which is typical of men in general. The gunmen's rage is taken to extreme measures, which underscores the level of frustration and rage innate to those individuals.[10]

I do not believe that religious people have been targeted specifically, though times have now changed, given the Israel-Hamas War. People find easy scape-goats to focus their rage. But neither do I believe that school children are specifically targeted by shooters. Instead, synagogues, churches, and schools have vulnerable people collected in one place, where one represents those who believe in God (synagogues and churches), where one's belief in God can help people to deal with tragedy. This may be something that a gunman lacks. Additionally, targeting children destroys parents' futures, something again that gunmen commonly lack, given that they are often killed or commit suicide, demonstrating that they saw their future in death. This is sad.

However, I believe that working toward a future where everyone benefits should be on the minds of all members of our society, since there are some who overly benefit from the system as it is, whereas there are those who do not benefit from it at all. When the vast majority of people do not benefit from society, as is the case now, given the rising costs of so many goods after Covid restrictions have subsided, then we need to be watchful for *more* ways that people will manifest violence, not fewer. We should also be on the look-out for how people will "squeeze" others for more money for services, even when there is no call to do so. Until the economic picture stabilizes for a majority of people, which I believe will happen, though not immediately, we should brace for situations becoming worse before getting better. Flexibility after Covid has been a gradual realization.

---

[9] See Mark Follman, "What Drives Mass Shooters to Kill," *The Week*, June 3, 2022, p. 12.

[10] See Appendix A for a discussion on aggression in general.

Security concerns still outweigh flexibility.

Economic Stability

The "Great Resignation" has now given way to something like a recession, which has prompted lay-offs—at least this is how I read it, though there is news of positive job growth. In other words, the time when workers could call the shots still exists in some quarters, but it will not last forever. Airlines are now reaping great profits, but they are also training new personnel for jobs in the industry, especially pilots, who garner significant salaries. Air-traffic controllers are in short supply due to a lack of retention and recruitment, but also because the job is difficult and requires steady focus. This situation and others will stabilize, but they will take time. Automakers have received the chips that they needed, so that their production-lines can stabilize. Supply lines will open up again as new workers drive trucks, though these workers have come from atypical areas of the population, which is also true within other industries. In general, there is a re-shifting going on in the country, but everyone will pay for such a shift to occur. Volatility is currently the word of the day, but stability will again surface. When will this take place? That is unclear. But these are matters that are largely centered in the US, which will impact other nations as they impact us. However, I would suggest that the most volatility will relate to China.

China's former no tolerance lockdown policy in relation to Covid has crippled its trade. President Xi has attempted to win back trade partners by his visits to various countries. Once again, the inflexibility of companies to "set up shop" in other locales stands in the way of realizing smooth transitions to other manufacturing opportunities, which will not be as volatile as in China. Many tech companies have carved out niches in India, providing their own infrastructure as up-front costs, given India's lack of such. I cannot assess what start-up costs would be in India, but India's technological know-how is currently under-utilized and under estimated. The US could benefit more from such partnerships.

Local > National > Global

I think that many people recognize that border security and the sovereignty of the Nation are important, but national issues are one thing, whereas local ones are what matter to most people.

I have lived in the inner city of Baltimore. Despite its reputation, even today, I believe that people can go about their business safely, frequenting restaurants and doing shopping. But Baltimore's reputation, which is a transcendent understanding, is overarchingly negative, so people have told me more often than not how they will not travel there anymore, though they once lived and frequented there. A murder and a knifing occurred around the corner from the rectory where I lived in downtown Baltimore, but I still felt safe. Fear, especially related to their personal safety, can cause people to view things negatively. Such an attitude catches on. The negative, especially in groups, will often obfuscate the positive. How deep one's values go will determine whether someone remains within a group, but also whether a person will visit a city.

I am aware of the number of murders in Baltimore that occur there each year, but I have personally never experienced any type of problem to my person. But unless people's attitudes change in relation to a host of matters pressing upon all of us: the economy, the war in Ukraine, the Israel-Hamas War, and others, then we will not be able to overcome our fears, because we will be too busy stoking their flames, thereby using our energy to promote fear rather than positive solutions. Additionally, the solutions offered and effected to address problems will not be as impactful if the "fear factor" were not involved. People need to take risks and engage in the practice of placing faith in other people, circumstances, and things, otherwise fear and the energy expended toward it will sap the ability of more and more people to transcend situations in a positive way, as we currently see occurring within our society. But this leads to why we discussed transcendence and how it coheres with faith-based considerations, which typically have to do with religious understandings.

Faith

I have laid out how a forensic sense of things can break them down, so that we can examine the pieces of something that we are attempting to study. This is great in medicine, the law, science in general, mathematics and other fields. But transcendence taken in a positive direction can bring parts together to form wholes that are greater than their sums, because of an esprit de corps or something similar. A team is made up of a group of individuals, but individuals must cohere through synergy to accomplish something. Transcendence in a positive direction delivers success to such endeavors. When athletes or musicians or people learning something spend their time on these occupations, they grow beyond their current horizons, which is a transcendent act. God, I would submit, is the ultimate Transcendence, which draws people to do things that they wouldn't necessarily do, but it corresponds with our discussion of transcendence.

God

I am not concerned with arguing about the existence of God. That is a forensic question. I am instead arguing that believing in God can take a person beyond him or herself as any relationship would, but then, because it is God, it takes a person even beyond human concerns. People can argue against this point, which even I can attest to, that even believers in God can do heinous things. This is true. But just like non-believers can perform heroic acts, I am suggesting that belief in God and religious understandings *in general* are meant to draw people beyond themselves into the realm of altruism, where people are concerned with doing what they can for their fellow human beings. All of us know how to address our own needs. We are usually adept as well with addressing our loved ones' needs. But religious training is meant to carry us even beyond these limits.

I'm not sure that anyone would argue that helping others in their time of need is a bad thing. Religious people tend to have clearly identified boundaries for whom they help and why. These may be problematic for non-believers to appreciate, given the intricacy and nature of certain religious systems, but they are meant to guide people's lives, so that they are in line with their understanding of God's will for them. These values also help to appreciate right and wrong in their relationships with their neighbors. They can often spur people on to provide for others' needs.

If, however, we cast aspersions against certain groups, religious or otherwise, then we are engaging in character assassination, which is a negative form of transcendence. This is a powerful weapon that people use against others, but, again, it saps the finite energy that people have when they come together to accomplish something. Nothing will get done. Instead, I am suggesting that transcendence of the positive variety is something that everyone can share in, at least from some perspective or level, but its opposite, negativity, must be curtailed or the “nay-sayers” against projects will win out. This occurs not because they are “right,” but because they have not faced their fears and they are letting everyone else know it by their engagement in negative transcendence. Given the proclivity of (most?) people toward negativity, it is no doubt why such negative transcendence can gain momentum and undermine positive actions and momentum. Working in a positive direction often takes more energy than working in a negative one. This seems accurately to reflect human nature.

Political Views

I recently saw some political ads on television related to various positions. Spokespeople told how some politicians had sided with one position, making them “evil.” This is what is known as demonization: Painting someone else as evil, so that people will opt for the other side, even when they may not know what the other side is proposing or promoting. This is an effective method for undermining people’s credibility, otherwise people wouldn’t use it so often, especially before elections. This is the power of negative transcendence. Politics in general is about “taking sides.”

The problem is that there is no side to take in a discussion about the integrity of the power grid, for instance, or the economy. After all, it is negative transcendence that fuels fears on Wall Street, so that people sell their stocks “in a frenzy.” Keeping transcendence positive ensures stability, coherence, and mutual respect, among other positive values, whereas negative transcendence fuels chaos, animosity, fear, and a lack of accord. We could and should discuss approaches for addressing these issues, but there is still no side to take. But will people face their fears long enough and hold them—which is tension, but which is a transcendent act, because it involves risk—so that they can discuss a matter and evaluate ways forward without tipping their hats to fear? This is a difficult task to accomplish, but I believe that it is a necessary, but also possible one.

Critical Mass

Critical mass or a tipping point is when people move from one state of being to another. For instance, after studying for five years for a doctorate, I recognized internally that I was a "doctor," that is, I knew enough about my subject matter to be called an "expert," which is what doctor in this case means. I moved from being a student to a master, we might say. Nonetheless, there is a tipping point that is surpassed or a critical mass that is achieved to take a person or persons to that other level. It can also work in negative directions. *The Tipping Point* by Malcolm Gladwell states that smoking seven cigarettes per day is not an addiction, whereas smoking eight cigarettes is.[11] That eighth cigarette makes the difference: It is the tipping point. If there are more people who are in some state, for example, fear, than those who are courageous, then the "leading trend" will be in the negative direction. If it is the other way around, then things will move in a positive direction. Napoleon Bonaparte (1769-1821) is quoted as saying: "A leader is a dealer in hope."[12] True leadership depends on such a prospect, so that groups engage in positive transcendence and align their positive energies in a positive direction, otherwise negativity will win out. A plan, however, must be formulated in light of such hope, otherwise hope can go nowhere.

Hope

Hope is about transcendence, but I'm not sure that people recognize what it is and what it isn't. Again, from *the Week*, this time quoting Rebecca Traister from *New York* magazine, she relates the following.

> I am regularly asked about the temptation of hopelessness: 'How can we keep going when the progress accumulated over our lifetimes has been reversed?' But we go forward because that progress was made against forces that will never stop trying to reverse it. Despair is

---

[11] Malcolm Gladwell, *The Tipping Point: How Little Things Can Make a Big Difference* (New York: Little, Brown and Company, 2002).

[12] Patrick Lindsay, *Make the Most of You: 170 Ways to be the Best You Can* (New York: MJF Books, 2015), 90.

> poison. It deadens people when the most important thing they can do is proceed with more drive and force than they have [*sic*] before. Which is why the work ahead is insisting on hope, behaving as if there is reason for hope, even if you feel, based on the ample available evidence, that there is not.[13]

Traister's statement is poignant. Hope is an ability to recognize something more within a situation, when the facts actually point to depletion and therefore giving up. This can lead to a feeling of despair. Hope, then, is transcendent, where someone is able to see more than the sum of the parts that are arrayed before that person.

If we draw from the example above, then we can see that food and energy prices are high, but they need not lead in a direction of despair. Instead, we can place our belief or faith in a future that defies the logic of the situation. In the circumstances related above, this is not wishful thinking. Fuel costs impact transportation costs, which are passed on to food-producers. These are, in turn, handed on to consumers. There is a cause-and-effect relationship between fuel and food, so one should expect prices to rise. But, when supply and demand are in stasis again, which is currently not the case, because people are travelling due to the holidays and being cooped up for so long due to Covid restrictions. But people are also returning to work physically at their workplaces—at least some, though for two or three days, as people have informed me. Nonetheless, some prices should level out, after people return from their holiday vacations with family members. There is hope within this circumstance, but it is more logic. There is hope which recognizes a cause-and-effect, as presented above. But there is also hope when the people around us perform a hope-filled action or otherwise embrace positivity, leading to hope, when there is "more" than meets the eye. This is transcendence at a different level. Consider the following situation at a hospital in Kansas City.

> Fourteen nurses working in the maternity wing of the Kansas City Hospital recently became pregnant at the same time. Caitlin Hall, a nurse in the NICU and Labor

[13] The Week Staff, "Viewpoint," *The Week*, July 8/July 15, 2022, p. 12.

> and Delivery Department at St. Luke's East Hospital, was the first to tell colleagues she was expecting. After that, she said, "about every two weeks, someone else would announce, 'I'm pregnant.'" Hall gave birth to a daughter in June, and 13 more babies are due between now and December. It's been "really exciting to go through this season together," said nurse Ellie Kongs.[14]

Was this situation predictable? I doubt it. But one person's hope in having a baby became 13 other people's hope for having babies, too. But we could lose the sense of what we are discussing. The energy of hope had to be present as an energy propelling the couples into the future, which led to the pregnancies, *whether they recognized its presence or not.* If we were to examine this circumstance from a scientific worldview, then the situation would be unremarkable. But the power of hope is what is operative within this situation, as is the transcendence that it conveys. Pregnancy itself is a hope in the future for one's children, but it is propelled by the hope brought to the table by both parents which produces more than the sum of their parts. Again, we could reduce this to biology, but pregnancy is more than biology, especially within this unique circumstance.

Arrival

I believe that the film *Arrival* can shed some light on how time works with language in order to bring things to different ends.

> *Arrival* is a 2016 American science fiction drama film which stars Amy Adams as Louise Banks, a linguist enlisted by the United States Army to discover how to communicate with extraterrestrial aliens who have arrived on Earth, before tensions lead to war.[15] She is joined by physicist Ian Donnelly (Jeremy Renner) in her study.

---

[14] *The Week*, July 8/15, 2022, p. 12.
[15] *Arrival*. Directed by Denis Villeneuve. Paramount Pictures. 2016. https://en.wikipedia.org/wiki/Arrival_(film). Last updated 13 March 2024.

Twelve extraterrestrial spacecraft hover over various locations around the Earth. Affected nations send military and scientific experts to monitor and study them; in the United States, US Army Colonel Weber recruits Banks and Donnelly to study the craft above Montana. On board, Banks and Donnelly make contact with two cephalopod-like, seven-limbed aliens, whom they call "heptapods." Banks and Donnelly research the complex written language of the aliens, consisting of palindromic phrases written with circular symbols, and share the results with other nations. As Banks studies the language, she starts to have flashback-like visions of her daughter, "whom she will not have until some time in the future."

Donnelly discovers that the symbol for time is present within the message, and that the writing occupies exactly one twelfth of the 3D space into which it is projected. Banks suggests that the full message is split among the twelve craft, and that the aliens want all the nations to share what they learn.

Banks goes alone on one occasion to the Montana craft, and it sends down a transport ship. One heptapod explains that they have come to help humanity, because 3,000 years in the future they will need humanity's help in return. Banks realizes the "weapon" is their language, and learning it alters humans' linear perception of time, allowing them to experience "memories" of future events. Banks' visions of her daughter, Hannah, are revealed actually to be premonitions; her daughter will not be born until some time in the future.

Banks returns to the camp as it is being evacuated and tells Donnelly that the aliens' language is the "tool." She has a premonition of a United Nations event celebrating newfound unity following the alien arrival.

> In the present, Donnelly expresses his love for Banks. They talk about life choices and whether he would change them if he could see the future. Banks knows that she will agree to have a child with him despite knowing their fate: Hannah will die from an incurable disease, and that Donnelly will leave them after she reveals that she knew this.

Banks is able to recognize that the language that she is learning from the aliens permits her to encounter the past, present, and future, though this is a gradual recognition for her. Yet, she and her colleagues take the risk to engage the aliens due to their respective expertise. Banks is the source of the insight for recognizing the importance of what they are doing in engaging the aliens. But how do the present, past, and future converge in our lives in modern times that help us to appreciate them in a different light?

Crime

I do not have much fear about crime in my life. If it happens, then it happens. This may be a maverick approach, but it stems from never having been accosted or having anything major stolen, despite living in large metropolitan areas. I can appreciate that others may have had different experiences which may cloud how they view the inner city. Nonetheless, I know that I use strong passwords on my computer accounts. I have locks on my doors. I do not venture into problematic areas of cities. If I happen to do so, then it occurred when I was unaware. When I become aware, I quickly make a correction. To date, having lived in major cities for more than twenty years, I have never been mugged, assaulted, or had any other negative experiences. Others have experienced such things, so they must take further precautions, given where they live and other factors. People must take responsibility for their own situations where they can. No one can help people who will not help themselves. Crime that happens outside of inviting it is a different story altogether.

There are areas that are crime-ridden. Drugs often have a part to play in such locations as do organized crime and the like. I believe in first-responders, especially the police. There were something like twenty-five members of various law enforcement agencies who attended my last parish. I never felt unsafe there. But what kind of crime are we talking about, when we discuss crime in general? I believe that violent crime is what is on people's minds most.

Types of Crime

According to the evening news, violent crime is down in most major cities.[16] As stated above, I lived in Baltimore, which is known for its high murder rate. The number of murders has mostly decreased over the past five years, but it is still at an alarming rate.[17] I tend, and I know others do, too, to associate violent crime with drugs. I know of at least three places in Baltimore where drug dealers sell drugs. I would frequently pass one such location when I visited a priest at his church. I drove into this area, but I did not walk around the area. I remained with my friend within a fenced-in area enclosing his church grounds. I felt safe there, even staying overnight. But Baltimore in general terms is not wholly described by such a scenario. Even the inner city is safe, with some exceptions, which I learned through my own by observation. However, there was a police presence in all of the areas where I walked. I'm not sure what more anyone can do. There will always be some level of crime in a city or elsewhere.

When it comes to other types of crimes, not related to drugs, then I believe that the police should be empowered to handle these matters as they see fit, in concert with other officials. There have been difficulties in some locales, most notably Minnesota, where problematic police cultures exist. It goes without saying that those in leadership positions need to take corrective measures to address these problems. The City of Baltimore has had its share of problems from this perspective. But it has also seen its police ranks dwindle in recent years. It has low morale, according to current and former members of the force with whom I have personally spoken. Baltimore is attempting to diminish the benefits that police

---

[16] Ken Dilanian, "Most People Think the U.S. Crime Rate is Rising. They're Wrong." *NBCNews*, Dec. 16, 2023. https://www.nbcnews.com/news/us-news/people-think-crime-rate-up-actually-down-rcna129585.

[17] Baltimore Examiner Staff, "Baltimore Homicides: A 5-Year Analysis," *Baltimore Examiner*. December 25, 2023. https://www.baltimoreexaminer.com/baltimore-homicides/.

receive. This is an accident waiting to happen. It undermines morale and diminishes the esprit de corps among officers, so that others are unwilling to join the force, because leadership seems not to have their backs. The front-line of defense (first-responders) is tasked with patrolling the inner city, and the City of Baltimore is cutting their pay and benefits. There is no incentive for carrying out police work.

People want less crime. Who wouldn't? But I personally don't believe that there is a tried-and-true method for achieving this result apart from treating the police and other first-responders with respect and ensuring that they are receiving appropriate compensation and benefits commensurate with the risks that they encounter on a day-to-day basis. I rode along for half a shift with a deputy sheriff, attending his calls with him after applying to do so and being vetted. The deputy was 24 years-old, I believe, and had been on the force for four years. He was capable and did his job well, but I found him *young*. Nonetheless, I was grateful to him for his service and for his willingness to have me accompany him. I wonder who will take his place or otherwise join the force? I don't believe that this is a trivial question. If, however, those in charge do not recognize that some forms of crime will increase, not decrease, in years to come, then I believe that they are short-sighted. Budgetary concerns are important, but they are not the only ones to consider. The values that faith-based lives imbue are foundational for how people conduct themselves with regard to morality. They tend to stick with these values throughout their lives. Those whom I know who base their understandings related to right and wrong on ethics, oftentimes bend with the winds of change. There is always a need for flexibility, but human nature seldom changes unless something holds it in check. The path of least resistance is typically a prominent force to reckon with, unless someone has already contended with it. This is an important point.

Conclusion

Our initial inquiry has assessed various contrasts using the ideas of flexibility and security, where flexibility indicates how much leeway a person or group or entity is willing to give in sharing one's core values with others. On the other side of such an assessment is the level of security that dominates a group, where security means the maintenance of one's boundaries and the dance that goes on at the peripheries to protect access. These are not easy dances to effect, yet they do occur frequently. The adept leader is one who can perform in such a way that leaves participants with a positive sense in relation to this experience.

Though rejection of new members for a group may occur, there is no need to devalue others in delivering the verdict that a person who wishes to become a member is not a good fit. Our society has sometimes disrespected others using an “us-and-them” strategy, which has worked in the past, but cannot be a viable way forward any longer. This strategy works in some areas, such as professional athletics and military engagements, but it does not work in cases where a group is dying, but its core members seek to keep the group going in a healthy manner. Instead, a different strategy seems to suggest itself, where respect for everyone involved is the order of the day. Respect is a term that can dance with both flexibility and security.

But what does respect look like? Respect is a transcendent understanding, which can be either positive or negative, depending on the circumstance. The stock market rises and falls because of transcendence in either direction, but what can push the process to achieve critical mass in the other direction? Demonization is one technique that is used within politics, but sometimes there are no sides to take. Real problems like the economy and those related to the power grid or additional sources of energy do not have any sides. These are huge problems that require people working together in a positive way so as to tackle these thorny and complex issues. If too many people are taking sides, then they aren’t directing their transcendent energy in the direction of a solution. We all know that this is the order of the day.

Flexibility and security also relate to crime. Crime will occur, especially where there is a lack of people taking proper precautions. When proper precautions are in place, then crime is more difficult, which, it seems to me, is what most of us should be concerned with. At another level, however, some believe that scapegoating police is helpful in the long run. I wholly disagree. Police are typically the first line of defense for fighting any sort of crime. Some locations have low police morale due to budget cuts. Places like the City of Baltimore need to rethink their priorities. I do not believe that Baltimore is unsafe, but its reputation is so inclined in this direction, that many people have told me that they no longer go there for any reason, though they once lived there. This is sad. I believe that there will always be some form of crime operating in pockets within most communities. Its total eradication is virtually impossible.

How does a person tip the scale in favor of a brighter perspective? This is where hope comes in. Leadership is key. Can leaders change attitudes? I believe that they can, but they must recognize transcendence, both how it works and how one must rise above the fray. Problems are complex. The most important problems do not require sides; they require rechanneling fear to work out viable solutions. Break down the sides' concerns over their fears and typically people can see answers on display, maybe not to all of the complexities, but at least some perspective may emerge that helps to make the problem less complex, but also clearer. Sir Charles Antony Richard (Tony) Hoare (1934 –) is quoted as saying: "Inside every large problem is a small problem struggling to get out." It's time we looked for positive solutions and positive transcendence, so that we can address the enormous problems that plague us as a Nation. Such an undertaking can itself lead to hopelessness. Instead, positive transcendence can help to turn things around.

Chapter 5 will discuss some of the issues associated with education. Since education is mandated for all, it seems an appropriate area to consider from many different angles.

5 THOUGHTS ON EDUCATION

I once tutored a student, a junior in high school, who had been suspended from attending school. We met at a public library for the duration of his suspension, which was about two weeks. He was mostly faithful to attending the sessions. He shared with me that his guardians had told him that attending high school didn't matter. They had been successful in their lives without education past high school; he could do the same. We worked on his assigned school work for a time, until he announced that he would be leaving school in order to pursue a GED. We then looked at the curriculum available in the library for completing the GED.

This scenario can obfuscate something important if we let it slide and that is the contention that one's educational performance does not matter, and that a GED is sufficient to make a decent living in today's society. For some, this may be the case. Several factors can contribute to how to weigh prospects for people. But a lack of initiative or ambition can also undermine one's future just as readily as a lack of academic success or pursuit. I believe that this, more than anything else, can hamper how society will promote the present generation into the future. We must consider the issues surrounding this scenario in earnest.

Believing In More than Loving

Most parents love their children. They would do anything that they could for them, oftentimes even to the point of heroic sacrifice. But will parents do what they *can't* do, and that is to take their children into the future in a manner that will lead to their children's *own* success? This requires permitting children to make mistakes, but in a controlled fashion, so that they can learn from this. School teachers provide significant role models in what this involves.

In general, school teachers permit their students to make mistakes, though they then step in to assist them in learning from those mistakes. Parents need to do the same with their children as lessons for them, so that they have experience doing what is wrong or problematic so as to learn from that experience. It can be difficult for parents to stand on the sidelines and let things simply happen. But children need to make mistakes, so that they can experience first-hand what it means to go from one "state" or experience to another. We call this growth. Parents may intervene too quickly or control problems to such a degree that their children never deal with anything substantial on their own. This is not helpful. Children need to grow in their ability to deal with problems in a gradual fashion, not go through life avoiding them.

In the scenario detailed in the introduction, the student's guardians told him that a GED would be sufficient to get along in life. This may have been true during the time when they made a living, but I'm not sure that this is true today. This does not mean that everyone needs a college education either, but it does mean that everyone in American society receives mandated education, so it ought to be embraced as fully as possible. This may not be easy, but parents need to encourage their children to go beyond their current limits and emotions, that is, the sense of not feeling like completing or learning something. From my perspective, parents are not truly *believing in their children into the future*, which means addressing and confronting attitudinal difficulties, when they do not require them to hold the tension of having to do things that they may not want to do. After all, no person on the planet does everything that he or she wants to do all the time. Sometimes we step away from doing anything at all. But, more often than not, most people rise to the occasion of doing what they need to do, so that things get accomplished, but I would suggest that even this strategy requires instruction.

Parenting/Teaching for Success

Teaching and parenting ought to go hand-in-hand, so that both parties are on the same page. Pedagogical methods are also the best for parenting, which means that parents ought to teach their children how to address problems in a gradual way, but they should also model such behavior to their children and not stand in the background without highlighting what parents are doing for them. By sharing methods for success, such as organizational skills and becoming articulate, parents can demonstrate through their own example how their children ought to conduct themselves in fostering such skills. When parents and teachers adopt similar strategies, then children will receive reinforcement in the home *and* at school, which can only help to develop the intended skill or skills.

What can happen, however, is that parents leave all matters pertaining to school in the hands of school personnel and teachers. Instead, I believe a partnership ought to develop, so that, for instance, parents check students' homework and teachers provide feedback both to students and parents. Within such a structure, children recognize the importance of responsibility and accept the challenge, recognizing that there is accountability both in the home and at school. Being consistent ensures that good practices are realized, that is, made real through us in students' lives.

Frequently students will ignore school work in favor of activities that they enjoy doing, such as playing video games or using smartphones. The ubiquity of these devices is clear, so prohibiting them entirely would be problematic and could cause resentment. Instead, from the outset, parents ought to identify time limits for using such devices and follow through with how long their children use them. Verification and consistency with such a process are important aspects of ensuring that students complete their school work, but also that they follow parents' directions, thus reinforcing respect for them.

Parents must also make the effort to ensure that they serve as good role models with their own use of electronic devices, especially smartphones. By limiting their own usage, parents demonstrate through their own example that overuse of devices can diminish people's ability to interact with others in a manner that leads to deeper social relationships. By encouraging friendships, play dates, and other social activities, parents can help their children not only to be successful in academics, but also in the social development that an education is meant also to foster.

Federal Education Laws

The No Child Left Behind Act (NCLB; 2001) and subsequent federal legislation (Every Student Succeeds Act [2015]) have made it clear that education supported through federal funding is a prime initiative within our society. Educated people fare better all the way around in life. Our culture, by enacting, supporting, and enforcing these laws, underscores the value of education for every citizen. It even provides for interventions for children early in life, so that they can receive assistance if they have a disability, which can follow them throughout their academic career, at least until they are 18. This, too, says something about the culture of our society, when Americans with disabilities are accommodated through physical changes to buildings and other similar modifications that lessen the burden that societal structures can bring about when such matters are ignored. I have travelled overseas where such assistance does not exist and I have noticed that people with disabilities, for instance, those who need a wheelchair, cannot get around due to limitations within buildings or on walkways. It took time to implement such changes in this country, but we now mandate accommodations for people with disabilities, so that they can get around more easily when new buildings or construction is planned. Planning can help to accommodate people with disabilities, which works toward helping people to be successful.

Our system of education also fosters assistance for students with disabilities, so that they, too, can develop in their own ways, so as to maximize their functioning, intellectual and otherwise, within society. There is a limit to such assistance, but basic helps are in place to ensure that students can realize their potential.

Education Assistance

Initiatives exist that have not so much questioned the rights of students to an education, but have attempted to apply them in a broader sense than the manner in which they were envisioned. One need only consider students who may lack documentation for citizenship due to immigration status. The Supreme Court, in its ruling against actions by the State of Texas (*Plyer v. Doe*, [1982]), ruled that even undocumented students are entitled to the same educational rights under the law as students who are citizens.[18] Such students must prove that they live within a specific community in order to qualify for educational services in that area, but proof of residency is a far cry from proving citizenship.

Accommodations for Language

From another perspective, the State of Arizona has wrestled with the issue of language within that state, namely, how teachers can accommodate the many languages that they meet from the students enrolled in its school system. Educational legislation, specifically *Lau v. Nichols* (1982), virtually mandates bilingual education, though subsequent legislation has questioned if this is actually the interpretation of this law.[19] Be this as it may, it does seem as though children's language ability must be taken into account in order for them to advance and succeed within an established curriculum. I appreciate many different aspects for scrutiny that can implicate how such students will fare.

Multi-Faceted Understandings of Language Learning

I have learned seven languages in my life. Modern languages require different skills from ancient languages, given that ancient languages, such as Latin or Biblical or Ancient Greek, require the student to learn forms passively, that is, for recognition purposes only, because they will be used solely for reading, not produced for speaking. Similarly, vocabulary is learned, not for speaking, but for recognition within a text for understanding that text. This type of learning becomes passive over time, meaning that ancient languages are recognized, whereas the other aspects of language production—writing and speaking—do not occur.

---

[18] U. S. Supreme Court. *Plyer v. Doe*, 1982.
https://www.law.cornell.edu/wex/plyler_v_doe.
[19] U. S. Supreme Court. *Lau v. Nichols*, 1974.
https://supreme.justia.com/cases/federal/us/414/563/.

In contrast, modern languages require a different skill set, because people must produce forms on the fly, that is, extemporaneously, and further comprehend what people are saying, writing, or conveying through reading. This is a much more robust and multi-faceted process. Thus, speaking, reading, and writing are skills that are necessary for modern language acquisition, whereas only reading knowledge is necessary for ancient languages. This will serve as a model for appreciating how even modern languages can become passive to learners, though in a different manner.

Meta-Language

I have met children who could speak multiple languages. I consider their approach using the following metaphor. They were taught to speak multiple languages at an early age, but they were able to recognize their own thought-patterns and then express them through multiple linguistic means, which, of course, had to be learned. They did this unconsciously. Of course, one's language and culture color the articulation of one's thoughts, but these children had some mastery over their thoughts, so that the means for articulating them was determined by the needs of the person whose language that they knew. We can appreciate these circumstances as exceptional.

For most of us, we learn our first language in bits and pieces at home, not systematically. There are milestones as we develop language skills, but the systematic process of language acquisition typically occurs in school. From such a perspective, Arizona, as one example among many, is right to emphasize language acquisition (reading, writing, and speaking) from grades K-3, since this is the crucial time when children are ripe for developing language skills.

But we should consider that school is only one place where such acquisition can occur. Playing with friends and communicating with them also offer other opportunities for this to take place. Television may be another source, as books may serve such a purpose as well. Parents or other family members reading to children and speaking with them can offer additional opportunities for language acquisition. If the language at home and that at school are different, then, I suppose, this can be confusing to children, though it can also expand the language learning for the child in both languages.

However, my experience has been that English will dominate over time even if a student has earlier learned another language, because English is the language being emphasized systematically in school, whereas one's home language will typically fall into passive understanding and/or learning. Forms of one's home language are typically not learned systematically, so that children do not gain literacy in their original language, whereas they do in English. This can be viewed in both positive and negative terms, but I believe that the overarching positive component bodes well in the long run. The English language is the dominant tongue in America. Learning it well can help children's future success in many different ways, most especially tying into the cultural system that English transmits, which also implicates the value system that it carries forward with it.

Immersion

Arizona has adopted an immersion program in the English language for students whose first language is not English. Immersion can be off-putting and confusing at first. It can cause stress for those who must be immersed in it. However, social interactions among children as well as the structure of the language are being taught at the same time, which can help to minimize the negative effects of learning English as a second language (ESL). Additionally, all students are having the same experience, which is helpful in itself. Common struggles help people to cope with difficult situations, as well as come together.

When I have learned languages as an adult, I could recognize that immersion would not have worked for me, because I appreciated my own need to understand the structure of the language first to guide my learning of the target language. The structure (grammar/vocabulary) served as a scaffold, so that I could develop further skills, based from my understanding of English, though language learning also helped me to learn English better. The earlier in life that language acquisition occurs, the less painful the learning process will be. Given children's proclivity toward language acquisition in their early years of school, they do not need as much scaffolding. Instead, linguistic structures develop as they go along through their learning. Admittedly, as children or adults get older, it becomes increasingly more difficult to acquire a new language. Nonetheless, speaking, reading, and writing the new language must still be practiced or, as with anything else, these skills will dissipate through lack of use. Practice makes permanent.

Loss of First Language

I have assisted many adults with ESL. They have all been literate in their first language. In general, they communicate with family and friends in their native tongue. They had their own reasons for learning English. However, for those who are school-age when they learn English, these students commonly lose their ability to remain articulate in their original language due to a lack of systematic instruction, but also dominance of English. Over time, the native tongue becomes a passive understanding, where children can understand what others are saying in the original language, but they cannot formulate their own responses in the native language over time. My own mother fit into this category. Typically, those who focus on the target language as children will develop a passive understanding of their original language, whereas they will become active learners in English. This is similar in scope to the learning of ancient languages as presented above in terms of active and passive learning. I know of some schools that are immersive in another language. I believe that such schools help students to retain these other languages for many different reasons. I applaud such efforts, since language acquisition is a great learning tool. Nonetheless, the education system for society at large must foster a standard of English to foster unity. Other vehicles can serve this purpose, but I do not believe that there is any as powerful as unity of language.

Cultural Assimilation

Some theories related to language acquisition discount the (gradual) loss of one's original culture through assimilation, as related above. I would suggest that this point deserves attention, which admittedly depends on many different aspects of a student's life. For instance, if the family with whom one resides speaks a language other than English, then practice in the target language will not be as effective, nor will it occur as often as when English is also spoken and/or practiced in the home. Practice determines one's mastery of English, but so does reinforcement by other people in the home or on the playground. Cultural "waves" tend to carry students in one direction or another, depending on the strength of those waves, especially the aspect of reinforcement. Language is a vehicle of culture. Learning English will cause some level of assimilation, but the level will be determined by how strong or weak the language and culture are in the home. Thus, assimilation is a sliding scale in terms of loss, which depends on many contributing factors.

Special Education and Language Learning

Some students who come to the US may have never been to school, so their experience within the US school system may be their first exposure to systematic education. Additionally, other school systems may have offered some level of education, but this did not serve to challenge these students. Be this as it may, educators can often mistake a lack of experience with formal schooling and its systematic requirements with a lack of intelligence on the part of the student, because he or she cannot keep up with English language learning or some other aspect of the curriculum. This need not be the case. Instead, students may struggle with English language acquisition because it is hard for everyone to learn another language, but also because they do not have formal skills for learning in general. They may also lack skills in applying themselves. Children's effort must be taken into account when evaluating how well they perform in language learning.

Yet, there is also the level of where students are in life, which I believe corresponds at least somewhat with Maslow's "Hierarchy of Needs" paradigm.

Hierarchy of Needs

Abraham Maslow (1908-1970) proposed that people develop according to a hierarchy of needs, which means that when someone is in survival mode, the lowest and most instinctive level, he or she will be concerned with food and shelter, so other concerns will be markedly less. As one's basic needs are addressed, a person is able to flourish more, which means that other values become more prominent.

As a point of comparison, people who move their residence within the United States, for instance, to take on new jobs, usually do so by securing their new job first, then moving their family to join them when the time is right. Thus, survival mode is operative, but it is handled usually by one parent, maintaining necessary structures in order not to lose one's standard of living, which is higher on the hierarchy of needs. Typically, one parent ventures out and the other parent "holds down the fort." Children moving into another school district will generally speak the same language, and the culture will be much the same from school to school, but they still have to make new friends and address differences in their new home life, etc. In the beginning of any transition, survival, getting around, and other basic concerns are in place and command one's energies and attention. Development at other levels will occur later, after one's basic needs are addressed.

Now consider when immigrants with no sense of English or American culture come to the US. Their first concern is presumably survival: Food and shelter at least, though a way to make a living, will develop quickly. If a circumstance brings a great deal of stress with it, then people will attempt to survive before anything else. Their survival concerns will be protracted in comparison with the scenario above. Their children, entering a school system, have to master English as well as watch their parents find work and housing. Such concerns stand in the way of "hitting the ground running," which can be the experience of many Americans. However, a failure to learn English within a designated time-frame does not mean that immigrant students are lacking in intelligence. Instead, it could mean that they might require more time to acquire English language skills due to such extenuating circumstances. Additionally, general educational requirements may be overwhelming for such students, who are being asked to learn a new language at the same time that they are pursuing the general curriculum found at the new school. Only the brightest of students could hope to succeed within such a situation.

Arizona's Language Standards

Arizona has high standards for language acquisition, but I'm not sure that they are realistic in relation to immigrants who do not benefit from their K-3 program of reading intervention. By this I mean that I am not sure that everyone can be brought up to speed within Arizona's targeted program of study, so that everyone achieves the ends for the curriculum. I mention this, not because I believe that striving and achieving are unimportant, but because I believe that there must be a realistic assessment of where students are in their language proficiency alongside their curricular performance in order to determine whether students can gain from the educational process in a positive, progressive fashion. I would assume that such an end would be exceptional, not normative, for the vast majority of students who enroll in school after K-3. This is not to say that their experience should not be maximized for them. I believe that goals and standards are important, but a "one-size-fits-all" plan will not deliver more than bilingual education, but then, students' relative "position" on a scale detailing their openness to language acquisition must be taken into account to determine the overall efficacy of such a program during students' academic careers.

Currently, as an educator informed me, students who are enrolled in a new school system are admitted to classes by their relative age, so a new student, who may be new to English, but is 14 years old, will be assigned to a high school curriculum, no matter that person's actual educational level. This puts an enormous strain on the system in a way that does not seem to help anyone in any substantive manner. It also impacts the students markedly. This matter requires further study.

Earlier, we noted that only the most gifted students could learn English *and* learn the curriculum at grade level. However, this is the current model being assigned to *all* students who are enrolled in school systems. Teachers must accommodate these students and their educational needs, which will typically not be at grade level, given their lack of familiarity with English, so they will struggle for a time. They may then become so frustrated that they may even give up trying to learn. This is a no-win situation for all concerned. The efforts of teachers are wasted. Student efforts are ultimately wasted as well. Administrators must simply say,

"Well, that's the policy." Such a policy is sad as it squanders tax-dollars at the same time that it wastes time and effort. A new model is needed, which appreciates students' circumstances and recognizes their frustration *and* the frustration of teachers. Would a parallel school that offers ESL in an on-going fashion for students serve them better? Would computer-based training (CBT) that uses on-line resources in multiple languages actually "meet students where they are" in a more apt fashion than a classroom specifically devoted to them in their own language? After all, student success will depend in great part on how well students learn English. There do not seem to be easy answers integrating immersion, ESL, and introduction into a standard curriculum. Bilingual education also seems not to be the answer. A new approach is desperately needed, given that so many immigrants are seeking educational opportunities.

Flores v. Arizona, 1992

The current Arizona appeal to the Supreme Court related to bilingual education (*Flores v. Arizona* [1992]), which has been on-going, is no trivial matter in relation to the issue of costs associated with education in general.[20] Arizona is wise to appeal this decision. In the interim, it has developed a method of dealing with language acquisition through immersion. This may not be the best option, but it is one based in research. This takes seriously the mandates of the Supreme Court and other courts, so that students benefit from the educational system as it is. This is important, because of implications from other mandates.

Students with Disabilities

Students with disabilities, as established by the Individuals with Disabilities Education Act (IDEA; 2004; 2015), *constitute approximately 30% of enrolled students*. This is a huge figure, when we consider that *everyone in America must be educated*. Nonetheless, after multiple assessments by a professional, each of these students requires educators to develop an individual education plan (IEP), so as to maximize these students' potential in the classroom. Such accommodations can be minor,

[20] U. S. District Court, *Flores v. Arizona*, 1992. https://azleg.gov/legtext/47leg/2r/summary/h.hb2064_02-27-06_astransmittedtogovernor.doc.htm.

such as giving a student more time to take a test, or major, such as providing a facilitator who follows the student from class to class. As with any large-scale measure, there must be a sufficient number of typical students to offset the expense for students requiring costly assistive measures. *But such measures should never detract from the success of the average student, since this would be unfair and overly implicate disability even above typical functioning.* Aiming to accommodate the middle or average student should be the norm, not either extreme, since extremes can serve to overburden any system. And yet this is where we are. Such a stance can lead to mediocrity, which cannot by its nature help to address the major concerns of our times.

Title IX and Education Support

Title IX is the name given to the initiative from 1972 that disqualifies educational programs from federal support funds if they discriminate on the basis of several factors: race, sexual orientation, sex, and others. Its original intent was literally to bring women onto the playing field, that is, to help them to participate in high school and other sports programs. This initiative propelled female athletes into the realm of competitive sports, which continues to this day. Few schools persevere if they lack sports programs. We can consider this legislation to have been effective in delivering what it set out to do: Namely, to ensure that people are not excluded from federally funded programs through discriminatory practices. This was and is a good initiative.

Discrimination as Neutral

Discrimination as a term related to legislation has a negative valence or connotation, which means that its intent is exclusionary in order to keep people out or down. However, people discriminate all the time in making choices about things. Some people like brown cars over gray cars. Some people opt for strawberry ice cream over chocolate. Options bring discriminations of various types, meaning that a person makes a selection in a positive sense over others. The selection process is neither right nor wrong within such a circumstance. Discrimination from such a perspective conveys a neutral sense, though people do not commonly use this term in such a way. It is, however, possible to do so.

I mention such an appreciation of a neutral sense because, from my studies in education, same-sex schools, which were first all-girls schools, were meant to help women to develop academically and in other ways apart from their (more dominant) male counterparts. After only a couple of months teaching in a grammar school, I could already see that the male students (K-5) were for the most part more aggressive by far than their female counterparts. They were more concerned with competition and in general demanded more attention due to behavioral issues. Such circumstances made me wonder, not whether to undermine or eliminate Title IX provisions, but whether we could further enhance its effectiveness through specific types of efforts that help students to develop and perform better, which means helping more students to be more successful. My own experience and study have also demonstrated that there are several different models of single-sex schools that function well in helping their specific populations of young men or women to develop better within those environments. However, it is also true that there are few current studies evaluating whether single-sex schools increase men or women's educational and other performance. What this suggests to me is not that we should abandon Title IX, but that we ought to examine whether Title IX's spirit should be fostered over its letter.[21]

The Spirit of Title IX

I am familiar with several of the cases related to education that support the letter of Title IX's intent. They are attempting to overcome discrimination in its many forms. Yet, I wonder if, in being so restrictive, we may be doing harm to the very population that Title IX was meant to protect, that is, women. I do not believe that anyone can answer such a point without studies being conducted that assess the matter within same-sex schools in comparison with co-ed schools of equal quality. Nonetheless, I do believe that the letter of Title IX should be examined, not to weaken it, but to recognize that not all so-called discrimination is the same. We need to encourage our children to develop within environments that help them to

[21] I am aware of the case, *United States v. Virginia et al.* (1996), related to the Virginia Military Institute's all-male admissions policy. https://library.law.hawaii.edu/2017/01/23/united-states-v-virginia-case-summary/. The proposal presented here is to underscore the need for further study.

grow in the best possible manner that *they* can. I am not advocating toxic masculinity or femininity in any environment. Instead, I contend that single-sex schools should not be barred from consideration as pre-emptively discriminatory, even at the public level, given that Title IX's protections have served and will continue to serve our educational system well. Nonetheless, I believe that its spirit can offer matter for further discussion and inquiry, so that both women and men can benefit more readily from the educational system available by national mandate.

Dyslexia

One of the most common forms of disability that I have encountered in my work as a reading interventionist is dyslexia. In general, students experience a disconnect between reading words, which may appear backwards in their minds, and associating meaning with them. This provides these students difficulties throughout their lives unless the condition is caught early enough, so that remediation is brought to bear, but also so that they can be assisted before they experience wholescale failure. These students are not "dumb." They have a difficulty that needs to be understood, assessed, and addressed through on-going support. I am aware of schools that specialize in teaching students with this condition. Their methodology is typically individual or small-group attention. Such schools are typically private and expensive, given the individualized attention that students receive. *Given that one in six people suffers from the condition*, we can appreciate how common the problem is, but we should also recognize the prevalence of great frustration on the part of students and teachers alike, especially within circumstances where the condition has not been identified or ignored for years.

Standardized Testing

Standardized tests can be used more to assist students in growing academically. However, they are more often used to assess the efficacy of the curriculum within a school system, which is related to rewards and penalties as noted above. I recently reviewed a standardized test, which would be taken by a second grader. It included recognizing the word "confound," which is not a word that any but the most gifted second-graders would know. Drawing from this example, I would conclude that the assessment did not seem to reflect the age of the students it was meant to evaluate. In my classroom, I used a book entitled *Dr. Fry's 1000 Words* for assessing where students are in their mastery of vocabulary in general. Kindergartners should generally develop a working vocabulary of 100 words; first-graders, 200 words; second-graders, 300 words; third-graders, 400 words; fourth-graders, 650 words; and fifth-graders, 1,000 words. The development from *learning to read* to *reading to learn* comes presumably during the third- to fourth-grade years. Nonetheless, whose standards were used to select the vocabulary for assessing student performance on this standardized test? From my cursory examination, it seems as though there is a disconnect between the test's identification of age-appropriate words and those of actual students, which implicates how funding is determined, but also how such assessments are used.

If the standardized testing actually corresponded with typical grade-appropriate milestones, then the testing would be useful on multiple fronts. Instead, it seems to be implemented without much direction or purpose, apart from funding concerns. This is a recipe for disaster, which we have already seen played out in countless school districts. Standards are needed to direct curricular decisions and actions, as is testing, but both need to be age/grade-appropriate and developed in consultation with professionals, following research- and standards-based developmental milestones. If these measures do not cohere, this legislation will not have the desired effect to assist students in making steady progress and realizing success. Instead, American tax dollars will have been squandered, as detailed below.

Alternative Educational Possibilities

Education is a government-mandated program, which has shown itself to be an utter failure in some locations in our country. A proposal to remedy this situation might be that if a certain percentage of students cannot pass state-mandated examinations with a passing score, then this circumstance would implicate an "audit" of the practices taking place in that school system. Given the enormity of such problems, any school that provides proof that its methodology can fare better than state-run schools would be permitted to receive federal funds for three years after which time the efficacy of their program would be evaluated through the same testing as other schools, namely, through state-mandated test scores. If the new school's students fail at similar rates, then they would forfeit future funding. If, however, they succeed in improving scores, then they could continue to receive federal funding. Private, religious, and parochial schools would all be permitted equal access to federal funding under such a mandate. Provisions related to discrimination would have to be assessed by a state board, but concessions would be permissible with the board's approval. These schools could also opt out of such participation or require their own testing methods to admit students. The breadth of services seen in private schools seldom rival those of public schools. Such disparities must be taken into account, not imposed upon systems wishing to help a national problem.

A court case involved students who could not attend public high schools given their paucity in the region where they lived in Maine. This necessitated their attendance at local private high schools. The Supreme Court ruled against the State of Maine (*Carson v. Makin* [2022]) for denying that state's education vouchers to parochial schools, given their proximity to the students involved.[22]

The practice of a parochial school receiving State funds was initially deemed unconstitutional by lower courts. However, the Supreme Court found in favor of the students, who chose to attend a nearby parochial high school. Such a precedent could support using federal tax dollars to assist other students who are underserved by current public education systems, but only when such circumstances were proven and demonstrable. This is only one idea for addressing this serious issue.[23]

An educator informed me that those who engage in home-schooling for their children can receive state aid for doing so in some states, which

---

[22] U. S. Supreme Court. *Carson v. Makin*, 2022. https://www.law.cornell.edu/supct/cert/20-1088.

[23] The case in Oklahoma, where the Catholic Archdiocese of Tulsa has attempted to set up a Catholic charter school funded wholly by the State, seems egregiously problematic. It is a reach on the part of the archdiocese to engage in what seems like a clear-cut violation of the separation of Church and State. See Murray Evans, "State Supreme Court Denies Walters' 2nd Bid to Intervene in Catholic Charter School Suit," *The Oklahoman*, Dec. 18, 2023. https://www.oklahoman.com/story/news/education/2023/12/18/walters-intervention-in-catholic-charter-school-case-denied-again/71967304007/.

permits another alternative educational opportunity for students. Some may gravitate in this direction, but this example could also serve to avoid dealing with the problems within public schools themselves. I am aware of individuals who home-school for a variety of reasons. It is a difficult choice to make and often involves an enormous expenditure of time and effort. I am also aware of many parents who pay for private school education for their children. These parents also do so for a variety of reasons. From my perspective, it is incumbent upon law-makers and school-board members to discover the multifaceted reasons that these parents have for choosing these other options, so that they can attempt to accommodate their needs in assessing the relative efficacy of their own educational programs. These parents generally pay twice: They pay their taxes as well as their children's tuition. A tax break of some sort could well be justified in such cases. The national mandate for education is failing these people, but I believe it is also failing others as well.

College Prep, Honors, Advanced Placement, and Gifted Students

From my perspective, when resources are rightly devoted to assisting disabled students, equal and proportional resources ought to be directed toward programs that assist students who are excelling with the curriculum. In my own study of education, I have found that the curriculum required for a Master's of Education lacked specific focus for helping above-average students achieve their potential, whereas there were many courses detailing measures to accommodate students with disabilities of various types. Educators who cannot challenge and guide above-average and gifted students place these students in jeopardy of not reaching their potential. This is the other side of the coin in relation to a discussion of disabilities, but I believe that it must be considered or the intent of NCLB or ESSA will have been undermined, which was mentioned above.

Other Vocations Outside of College Prep

I recall the speech of the valedictorian of my high school, who was two years ahead of me. Within her speech, she justified why she was not going to college, though she was graduating first in her class. Not everyone is destined for college or wants to go to college. Nonetheless, I believe that our curriculum in general has a trajectory in this direction. This is not without merit, but it tends to leave out a large segment of the population who do not wish to attend higher education.

The student whom I tutored, who chose to leave school and pursue his GED, wanted to get into the automotive field. Had he opted for this option earlier, he could have realized this goal through a vocational high school, where academics are paired with hands-on pursuits leading to a career after graduation from high school. However, it seemed as though he had been stream-lined toward the college-prep curriculum, because that was the default for anyone not knowing whether he or she would attend college. With a limited number of slots in some vocational programs, this model cannot be faulted, but we should note that this student was now considering his vocation later rather than sooner. I'm not sure that he is so different from others who question what they want to do with their lives.

Bennington, Vermont

I performed 15 hours of teaching observation of math teachers at a high school in Bennington, Vermont. I remained with teachers who taught college-prep courses. However, the entrance to the school led in two directions, since both the vocational and the standard high schools were housed within different wings of the same building. I am not sure how the two schools worked together—even whether they did. But I can imagine that students from one curriculum who find that that curriculum is not for them, could switch to the other curriculum. It seems that we call upon 8th-graders to know what they want to do with their lives at the age of 14. I would suggest that many will not know the implications of one skillset over another. Shadowing various occupations could offer an opportunity for appreciating such options, but I am at a loss for how to help students to recognize different career paths, apart from participating in such opportunities.

Other Careers

By giving a college-prep focus pride of place, we as a society can obscure other lines of work that may not require a college degree, though they do require specialized knowledge and "apprenticeship" to realize them. I am thinking of trades, such as those within HVAC or the electrical or other fields, though I am also thinking about individuals who perform master-level work, who are "a dying breed." Those who are masters of their crafts, who are creative within their specialized fields, have hundreds, perhaps even thousands, of hours of experience. For those individuals who are willing to devote themselves to such vocations, they should receive encouragement and assistance. Our society tends toward changing jobs frequently. The ability to remain within one line of work does not seem to be the rule anymore. Nonetheless, such individuals do exist, and they become masters of their respective crafts. I know some civil servants who are experts in their fields. My comments are meant to stir people to creativity in assessing their options for work, which can be both fulfilling, as well as lucrative, though specialized training is typically required. I further recall discussions related to aptitude tests that helped students to identify areas that they were either interested in or otherwise had aptitude for. Such tools could serve students in a positive fashion in an attempt to direct students toward careers that could suit them. This would also be an occasion where a so-called assessment would be used *for the benefit of students themselves*, given that such tests are not "graded" assessments, at least not in any typical sense.

First-Responders and the Military

Not everyone is cut out for every career. This is also true with regard to first-responders and those who serve our country in the military. In many ways, these two careers require a similar skill set, in that the training that one receives in general is going toward the situation at hand, not fleeing from it, where individuals attempt to assist others within what could be dire circumstances. It takes a special person, one who is often willing to put oneself in harm's way, to serve in such capacities. The reward for such experiences can be great, but it means devoting one's life—at least for a time—to develop the skills to assist others in this manner. This can truly be seen as a vocation.

I know of many individuals who have begun earning their living in the military or law enforcement. After achieving many years of service (typically 20), they switched to a different, though parallel, line of work. I do not recall hearing about such options when I was looking at the job market many years ago, but these seem like excellent opportunities for the right person.

The Road Less Traveled

All of us can be guided by the media or other influences to follow trends, attempting to capitalize on a "sure thing." But I'm not sure that there is a sure thing that applies to everyone's personality type anymore, as much as there is what can help me to feel fulfilled in life. Most people will claim: "I just want to be happy." I tend to disagree. I would suggest that most people want to be fulfilled. Our fulfillment is determined by the choices that we make and how much we throw ourselves into them, though also how we gain meaning from them. In doing so, we might find choices that are mistakes. But even mistakes—as presented above—can take on a positive sense with the right attitude. After all, it's great when you try something and recognize that it's not for you. We may not know what we will do afterwards and what will ultimately fulfill us, but we have learned what will not. This is something, which can also help to point toward something that will have a positive value in our lives, that is, something that will lead to meaning. I believe that meaning and fulfillment go hand in hand.

Conclusion

Since Americans tend to work for more or less 40 hours a week, we need to find something that can keep us going, if only to support us financially so that we can find fulfillment in other ways. Not every job is fulfilling for every person. Not every direction will suit everyone. These thoughts of mine are a meager attempt to recognize that everyone struggles with making choices, but educational concerns are a large piece of that puzzle. I don't believe that offering more choices is always a good thing, but if everyone is focused on only a limited number of options for their career choice, then the "smart" person would be looking for *other* ways to realize how to make a living. I believe that there are untapped options out there for people. We need to connect students with people who do those unique jobs or have those vocations with others who might consider that line of work if only they knew about it. Everyone wants to be fulfilled. I'm not sure if these words can lead in that direction, but that's where I have attempted to lead through them.

In the next chapter, we will look at economic concerns, which are matters that affect everyone in one way or another.

6 ECONOMIC CONCERNS

I recently moved my residence from Massachusetts to Delaware. I went to register my car. I was told that it will take about six weeks to bring this about. The teller, who was pleasant and kind, was up-front about the timeframe and the costs involved with the registration. The excise tax, which I had already paid in Massachusetts when I recently purchased the vehicle new, was 300% greater in Delaware than in Massachusetts. I would proffer that this is because Delaware has no sales tax, so it must obtain funds anywhere that it can, so it levies a tax on new cars. Taxes are taxes. My car insurance also increased. Massachusetts recently sought payment for excise tax again in 2024, though I have not lived in Massachusetts for six months. My insurance company in Massachusetts informed me that it was cancelling my insurance as of 1 February 2024. I must provide Massachusetts with proof that I have moved. There is something seriously wrong with these approaches.

I was working as a tutor for one business, but through two different contracts. Because of this, I was not eligible for benefits, since I technically do not work the 30-hour minimum within either entity to receive benefits through the company. Keeping costs down is how businesses remain profitable; I understand this. Personnel is the greatest expense for any business. I currently pay for my own health insurance, which is roughly $10,000 per year. I have not yet looked at the state-run health insurance system, because I required a name-brand drug. I can now pursue a different healthcare option, because this drug now has a generic version. I could not afford this and other drugs without healthcare coverage. We will examine healthcare matters further below.

Federal, state, county, and city governments raise revenues to fund initiatives. I recently paid my federal tax, as well as supplied tax forms for the three states where I have lived. If we are beneficiaries from such taxation, then we will not squawk as much when we have to pay taxes. However, if this is not the case, then oftentimes we will complain about having to pay them. But, from a wider viewpoint, we seek accountability in relation to taxes levied and spent, or else we will feel cheated in some way by these various levels of government. All of us seek "bang for the buck" when it comes to money that we have to pay into the system. I believe that people will not complain if their tax dollars deliver to them for a purpose, whereas they will not be pleased if they are misused, misappropriated, or squandered. This, I believe, is the dilemma that all of us face.

Federal Taxes

I pay into Social Security and Medicare through my payroll taxes like everyone else. These programs are good, especially for the elderly and those who have retired. I hope that I will benefit from them eventually, but I also appreciate that age requirements have changed over the years to accommodate that people are living longer. This makes sense. I am also aware of individuals who draw from the system due to disability or some other chronic condition. Again, I am fine with this to the extent that it is truly needed. In light of my father's death at an early age, my family was a beneficiary of these social programs.

But the tax code seems unwieldy and overly complicated. Many people benefit from tax breaks which are windfalls for them, whereas they do not pay taxes, which means that rank-and-file Americans have to shoulder the burden should more money be needed for various initiatives—tax hikes. I find this unfair. I endorse the government taxing legitimately and lawfully obtained earnings. Everyone, no matter who people are in life, ought to pay their fair share of taxes. I am not sufficiently aware of what all of the loopholes are within the tax code, but I believe that the code needs to be simplified, so that no one can take so many exemptions that his or her tax bill would be zero. A more simplified tax structure would offer incentives for businesses just as readily as for people who have write-offs, though I would suggest that business taxation is different from individual taxation. The *AARP Bulletin* that I recently received identified seven or so tiers for taxation, with increasingly higher percentage rates for higher earners. This seems more in line with an equitable system.

State Taxes

I lived in the Washington, DC Metro area for five years. I submitted my taxes there. When I moved to Maryland, the State of Maryland came after me for "unpaid" taxes, asking for proof that I had paid taxes to DC over the course of three years. I was surprised by this summons; I found it very aggressive. *I* had to prove that I had paid the taxes; it was not incumbent upon the State of Maryland to find the information about me. I was appalled, but had to comply. I ended up not having to pay anything to Maryland, but I found the situation upsetting and unnerving, because there was no way to question what the State of Maryland was doing.

States become desperate for the funds that they believe they are owed. This can make the State become adversarial. This is never a good thing.

County and Local Taxes

I've lived in counties in Maryland and the City of Baltimore, all of which require the payment of taxes for their jurisdictions. I'm not sure what services were being supported by these fees. Nonetheless, I paid them.

Sales Tax

Whenever we buy something, there is a tax added. Gas is taxed. Luxury items are taxed. Cigarettes are taxed with a "sin" tax. Of course, the sales tax varies from state to state, where Delaware has no sales tax, but there might also be a meal tax included, distinct from the sales tax. In DC, meal tax was 10%. There are occupancy taxes in motels and hotels. There are seemingly taxes everywhere that governments find to obtain revenue.

County Government

County government in Massachusetts has been eliminated. This is a great boon, though it causes me to wonder what those in county government were doing when it was in place, given that it is no longer needed.

More Funding

Everyone, including governments, wants more money. But I wonder if politicians recognize that those taxes for carrying out whatever service being provided to people come from the paychecks of regular people? I am not averse to paying taxes—to a limit—but I am averse to legislated taxes that are unclear in intent, or that only a few people benefit from. When I lived there, Maryland attempted to implement something called a "rain" tax, which forced even non-profit organizations to pay for their property holdings; the amount was determined by square-footage. The tax was eventually eliminated, but I am concerned that our governments have proliferated, which means that everyone wants a piece of the pie to advance their cause or perform their specific charge, but rank-and-file people have to pay the price. This has gotten out of hand to such an extent that, I surmise, most people question how tax-monies are collected and spent. We have reached a tipping point, where we don't trust any taxes, because there are so many. I wonder, in real dollars, how much people actually pay in taxes overall, when everything is considered. Have we achieved a level of taxation akin to France, as detailed below, without receiving commensurate services?

"Whatever the Market Will Bear"

The evening news reported that California recently voted in a measure that limits what insurance companies can charge as premiums, which led a company like State Farm no longer to do business in California due to so much regulation and its inability to make what it needs in order to run its business there. A regulatory move itself has consequences. Though Florida does not have such regulation, insurance companies' rates are now so high that some people cannot afford them. This is the other side of the coin. I attended a school board meeting in Massachusetts where the budget for the upcoming year was being discussed. The budget was limited by

Proposition 2 ½, which I recall from many years ago, limits the amount of funds that can be ear-marked for education to 2.5%. There are consequences to this action, which are true in every arena.

"Pure" capitalism cannot work, because social programs like Medicare and Social Security would not make sense from such a perspective. There's also a reason for Sherman Antitrust understandings, where monopolies that emerge must be dismantled, so that competition can take place to protect consumers. Socialist understandings cannot stand on their own, because, from my perspective, they promote complacency, which is the case in other countries. Too many taxes and fees, however, may be the case, but the question must be asked: What's the alternative? Regulation? That doesn't always work either. People want to be in charge of their earnings, but everyone out for him or herself also has its problems.

60% Tax Rate

I've been to France many times, where people pay 60% of their income toward taxes. This was the reason behind the recent upheaval there, when President Macron pushed through increasing the retirement age from 62 to 64 without popular support. The French pay so much of their income to taxes that they resented any change to their benefits from "the system." But, when push comes to shove, is America leaning in this direction in practice, because it is "hiding" the many ways that the various levels of government "take their cut" from a person's income? I do not believe that the comparison is without merit.

In effect, I suppose I am not overly concerned about taxes per se, because I know what I am paying from my tax return. I don't make that much money to have an accountant or someone else complete it.[24] Others may have different experiences. But I *am* concerned that I am being "nickled and dimed" around every corner, so that I end up paying a lot more in taxes and/or fees than meets the eye, with no appreciable benefit. (Any fee or tax is still a payment that I need to make.) I don't find this particularly fair

[24] I have used TurboTax in past years, but I used the Internal Revenue Service's on-line version for tax preparation this year. It worked well, asking many questions of me, so that I could maximize my refund or minimize payments. I was satisfied with this service, though its implementation of state returns did not seem as effective.

or upfront. For example, I appreciate the use of EZ Pass on toll roads. But I wonder where that money is going. I make my way from Maryland or Delaware to Massachusetts, which generally involves using the George Washington Bridge to get through New York City. I don't know how much it costs to use the bridge anymore, but is that money being used for maintenance of that thoroughfare or as a means for the City of New York to make money?

I'm not sure how I would address this issue, except to expose taxes and fees that are tacked on in bills. In large part, this already takes place when a person gets his or her bill at a store, though I don't know how much tax there is in the charge for gasoline or cigarettes. Nonetheless, I know that transparency could help to identify fees, as is true for credit card companies, etc., but this doesn't help with where the money is going. Accountability seems to be lacking, but so does consolidation of fees. Where do our dollars go?

Healthcare Costs

If we were to move toward universal health coverage, I believe that, over time, these costs would bankrupt the nation. I have no doubt of this, unless fees can be controlled from the outset, in a manner similar in scope to Medicare. For instance, under my current health coverage, I had an x-ray performed, which cost $700 total. I was responsible for about $500 of this amount. I was also contacted later for additional monies (around $20) to pay another fee. I mentioned my situation to someone who said, "Don't you have insurance?"—given the costs involved. The whole process took about 90 days to resolve. I don't understand why payments take so long. But I also have to admit that, had I known the cost up front, I would not have had the x-ray performed.

The problem was that, at the time, I had to pay the cost of two different insurance carriers: Health New England through my employer and Cigna through the Cobra plan from an earlier employer. Both plans identified costs of roughly the same amount each year. Cigna would have covered the x-ray 100%. Health New England would not. Why the difference? I would never have switched to Health New England insurance had I known that I was downgrading my services for the same amount of money. This is my take, though the services vary between the two. That's the source of the difference. Transparency could have helped me in this, but, instead, a general lack of transparency helped to keep me locked into these systems that shield costs from the consumer.

As another example, I was told by my primary care physician that I ought to get a colonoscopy. Given my experience with the x-ray, I didn't want to have to pay an exorbitant, out-of-pocket expense for this procedure, so I called the five telephone numbers that were required in order to find out what the fee for the procedure was. The person attempted to avoid telling me the actual cost associated with the procedure. She only said, "It's fully covered." I pressed her. She finally told me that a colonoscopy costs $6,000, as long as it is performed five years after the one before. I didn't press further.

$6,000 is a lot of money to me. I am told that the procedure involves a physician and two nurses minimum. It also requires a facility where such procedures are performed. It then requires clean-up services, etc. After everyone gets his or her payment, apparently $6,000 covers it. But I think that this scenario sounds a lot like taxes. There's one set fee, but there are a lot of people taking their "cut" from the pool of money, and no one's individual fee is identified for review in the grand scheme of things. Recall that it took five phone calls to find out the fee for the procedure. A lack of transparency is itself an ability on someone's part to charge whatever the market will bear, but when it comes to healthcare, it seems that a lot of things are papered over.

Conclusion

I don't make much money, but I do believe in paying taxes for some future services that I will receive, like Medicare and Social Security, but also for education, though I do not have children. But I wonder where the money is going when I pay sales tax, gas tax, meal tax, tolls, and other "hidden" taxes that aren't so clear. I wonder where the exorbitant fees that I am paying for healthcare are going. There is a seemingly deliberate attempt to conceal such information from those who pay these fees. I am not a conspiracy theorist. However, keeping matters concealed permits governments and insurance agencies and others to ensure that they can charge whatever they wish. This works against competition, because it forces consumers to pay what is charged rather than work to find the best price for the services that they are seeking. The current system does not seem fair. But how do we rectify it?

I don't have the answers, but I do believe that transparency could serve to help with finding a way forward. This is currently not the case. However small or large, transparency seems to be an aspect of our system that could use updating, so that costs are out in the open, not hidden from consumers' view. There's a reason why healthcare companies make it hard to find answers—and others, too. It's not about conspiracy; it's about making money, which is not necessarily a bad thing. The rank-and-file person will ultimately have to pay the bill. Transparency seems the only way to tip scales in the consumers' favor. It won't last for long, but it could push insurance and other executives into revealing how much they are drawing from consumers and how little they are delivering in services. Until such transparency exists, there cannot possibly be comprehensive healthcare coverage, because the same issues will exist within an already broken system, and companies will make the American taxpayer pay the bill.

Chapter 7 deals with foreign policy, though the chapter develops how both foreign and domestic policy measures implicate one another. In other words, the nation cannot be concerned solely with domestic matters and believe that international concerns are irrelevant. A full consideration involves both aspects.

7 FOREIGN POLICY

Foreign policy in a general sense is how the United States fosters relationships with other countries, oftentimes entering into treaties with them for specific purposes, which may involve trade, but also the ability to travel from one country to another and other matters. *The Constitution* associates the establishment of such treaties with the Office of the President. But it seems that, at least in recent times, foreign policy is problematic. *There seems not to be any policy in place*, at least this is how it currently seems to be playing out. If there is no plan, then there can be no control of borders, trade, and the other matters that countries share in with regard to their relationships. This seems to be our present state of affairs.

I would suggest that foreign policy directly impacts domestic policy, that is, the program of policies brought to bear to make the United States function coherently as a "country," which involves a myriad of interconnective components that help to run the "machine" that we call America. One need only recognize that the influx of migrants at the southern border of the country has gotten out of hand because no one has done anything to address this matter, but also because no one imposed measures to assuage situations prior to the crisis. In general, as with someone's personal health, addressing an issue early and treating it at that time, for example, cancer, can help to lessen the treatment that is required later on and its impact on the sufferer. We can all appreciate that we cannot plan for every occurrence in our lives. Sometimes human beings develop diseases which seem to come out of thin air. Nonetheless, we will use the sense that "an ounce of prevention beats a pound of cure." Using such a model as a metaphor for foreign policy, we take it as a verisimilitude that when crises so-called are less severe, we can devote fewer resources to help to alleviate them at the present moment. Instead, however, it seems as though we have turned our backs on maintaining relationships and have engaged in insular actions, pretending that there will be no ramifications on the international front. From such inaction, we have not dealt with issues at an international level, for example, immigration, in a concerted manner beforehand, so we must now not only develop a coherent policy for the future, we must also handle the thousands of immigrants who have already flooded into the country. This is a recipe for disaster.

This is but one example of a lengthy list of concerns that have gone unaddressed for quite some time, which have far-reaching implications for our country. We shall describe some measures to address them, not from an avuncular, condescending air, but from a sense of one possible approach. It remains to be seen whether measures can be brought to bear to address the chronic, unsustainable, and systemic problems that currently face our nation. The following are a few ideas to consider.

Central and South America

The "war on drugs" has raged on for decades, with countless resources being devoted to this important concern primarily in Central and South America. Drug cartels run much of Mexico and influence how the government of Mexico conducts its affairs. People are fearful for their lives, given the extent to which the cartels protect their business prospects. Powerful people enjoy lives of great wealth and privilege through the sale of drugs. Rank and file people do not benefit from the sale of drugs, but these same people are afraid of the cartels, because they will stop at nothing to ensure that their business operates, even to the destruction of whole families who cross them or otherwise thwart their efforts.

Other countries in Central and South America have become dictatorships, whereas others have limited rights and resources to assist their own people. Because of such conditions, people are fleeing their countries and coming to the United States in record numbers. These countries cannot support their citizens, meaning that socialist and other programs have not worked, and there aren't a lot of jobs for people to earn decent wages. In light of these conditions, people leave everything behind for an opportunity to come to America, often at great personal and financial risk and expense, even paying "coyotes," who prey on them, to assist them in their endeavor to seek a life of prosperity in America. The prospects in America seem superior to what they are currently experiencing. In other words, these people see hope in America, whereas they do not see such in their own countries.

When Not So Dire

When situations were not so dire, the United States had the ability to assist some governments, so that their countries could grow and develop. American investors could also have developed business ventures in these countries, so that people would have work, the single most important aspect of any "assistance" that the US could offer. Without work to make a living, people flounder. Socialist programs can only go so far.

Such measures, when evaluated in the moment, may seem like a waste of resources on our part, unless we take a look at what is transpiring today. Because there are no opportunities in their countries, people are fleeing in record numbers to avoid the poverty and desperation that their economies bring for them. Had businesses, foreign and domestic, offered people jobs *in their countries*, then these workers would be reluctant to leave. Of course, this assumes a host of cause-and-effect economic factors, but when economic and other supports are lacking, when one does not address difficulties early on, then these unaddressed problems will snowball into greater difficulties. This seems to be the origin for the situation that we have today. People are desperate, and they take desperate measures to flee their country, unless they have a reason to remain there.

Stop-Gap Measures

We might consider permitting countless migrants to enter the US to find work. Over time, I believe that this would be disastrous. Sanctuary cities will eventually exhaust their limited resources, because there are few to no provisions to permit migrants to work in the US, which they must be permitted to do over time. Additionally, those who do work will not be contributing much to the tax rolls, so social services will also be overwhelmed over time with contributions lessening and those who use these services increasing. We need to find a way of limiting the number of migrants who enter the country, but also to find a manner of "processing" them that permits them to work and to function in relative dignity. I believe that too many people believe that once migrants cross our borders—and this is tacitly accepted—they will become gainfully employed and adequately housed within a brief amount of time. This does not appear to be happening. Unless and until these sanctuary cities develop "plans of attack" for dealing with the flood of migrants, their citizens as well as the migrants will suffer. Those who bury their heads in the sand are contributing to the problem, which needs people who can make concerted efforts *to move from crisis, to survival, to maintenance, to flourishing within a reasonable amount of time* for migrants. Then and only then can people be concerned with citizenship and other like matters.

This is how foreign policy directly impacts domestic policy. All players in the game must be ready to come to the table to discuss policies and resources in clear-cut terms, otherwise *everyone* will suffer. I'm not sure that anyone wants such a development. The nay-sayers can live in their "dream world" of denial, but they are doing no one any favors by doing so, nor are those who follow them to the detriment of everyone else. This is negative transcendence as detailed in an earlier chapter.

Immigration in General

Most people are willing to undergo some form of graduated steps to enter the US legally and ultimately gain citizenship. Some may refer to migrants as "illegal aliens," but I would contend that migrants want to follow a process, whatever that is, for achieving citizenship. The evening news indicates that the current government-provided "app" is consistently inaccessible, because so many people are attempting to connect to it to enter their information. Many (if not most) migrants have smart phones, so the traffic that these systems are receiving must be enormous. This entire process needs to be ameliorated.

But, as I understand it, there is also a lottery for the already established slots that are offered to foreign immigrants each year. A recent provision from the Executive Branch has permitted many people from Venezuela to enter the country, bypassing the lottery system already in place. This seems like an unfair allowance for people from this particular country. People in Central and South America, but other places around the world, should also have access to the lottery system.

But we should also recognize that not all immigrants have skills that could benefit America. Some immigrants offer the US great resources, both personal and financial, given the line of work that they have pursued or will be pursuing. India has great educational institutions, some even rivalling similar ones in the US. By accepting more immigrants who offer greater skills to the workforce, we are building up the “brain” power of America. This can help both the tax rolls and the academic resources that the US can bring to bear to solve its problems. Competitive slots for immigration are not always fair, but when we examine what we are doing now, I’m not sure how much worse it can get, when we are letting virtually anyone into the country and permitting them to stay without much supervision or oversight. Such a policy does not offer them or the US much benefit.

Education Assistance

The children of immigrants are granted the same educational resources that any other child receives, as established by the Supreme Court. (See above.) The number of students in some areas has placed huge burdens on the school systems where these children must receive an education. Where school districts at one time were simply concerned with general resources, which is one level of concern, they must now be cognizant of the educational needs for students whose language of origin may not be (and probably is not) English.

I will not repeat statements pertaining to education that I have already penned. Nonetheless, I have worked with students in kindergarten through fifth grade to assist them with their reading, though most of my students were in K-2. Immersion into English must be engendered, as presented above. This is not to disqualify students’ languages of origin or otherwise discount their cultural heritage. However, I believe it a clear assumption that student success in general involves how well students learn English and learn other subjects through its use in the US. This means ensuring that students speaking another language are brought up to speed in English within the systematic learning environment that schools offer. I personally offer "reading intervention" with a view to ensuring that students become successful over time at their grade level. My services serve to piggy-back the instruction that they already receive within the structure of the classroom. These particular students need extra help, so that their educational experience will not cause them to flunk out, but also so that they do not resent their educational experience and leave school prematurely or otherwise not devote themselves to it. The longer that individuals remain in school, the better the prospect for success when they leave school.

Summary

The course of our discussion on immigration has moved from Mexico to drug cartels to Central and South America to immigration to education, which implicates resources, both financial and personal. It has further involved social services and what the US needs to do to meet its obligations both foreign and domestic, but also what it identifies as lasting measures that will bolster not only the people who make their home here, but also the economic base that, as a matter of course, should always be considered within such discussions. I am concerned for both the resources needed to handle the influx of immigrants, as well as the many social systems that are already in place that fight for those limited resources. Texas' actions to relieve itself of caring for so many migrants may not be politically correct, but it betokens unanswered needs that it has expressed on many occasions.

Be this as it may, one of the points of our discussion was to confront the suggestion that foreign policy should be considered in marked distinction to domestic policy. Such a contention seems absurd. Instead, there are implications for choices related to foreign policy that directly impact the resources that the US can offer in support of its citizens. Immigration seems to be the most obvious policy that people recognize as impacting them as rank-and-file Americans. I am not endeavoring to solve the crisis of immigration. Instead, I am attempting to draw attention to this area that needs people to form partnerships that can move us forward in addressing this complex issue.

Israel-Hamas War

The evening news is replete with story after story that demands that Hamas return the hostages that they have taken captive. However, the devastation that Israel is bringing to bear on Gaza is to such an extent that it should cause pause for whether it appropriately corresponds with the obvious atrocities of Hamas. Has Israel engaged in practices that many could call atrocities at this point in their military engagements? I can appreciate that people want their loved ones returned. But I also wonder how much greater would have been the devastation of Gaza had Hamas not taken hostages.

Ukraine-Russia War

The Ukraine-Russia War has largely faded from view, except for the personal appeal from President Zelenskyy for the US to continue providing aid toward its war effort. It should not remain unstated that Russia's advance into Ukraine caused both Finland and Sweden, who border Russia, to appeal to NATO for admission. Both countries are now members. They can see the writing on the wall that they, too, could fall prey to Russian expansion if they remained in isolation outside of NATO support. Support for Ukraine has been expensive; this is true. But lack of support for Ukraine could cause it to fall into Russian hands. The question is whether such support will bring about something for the US. In the long run, the answer is yes. In the short term, the answer is probably no. I believe that we have to take a longer view of matters to realize implications.

European Allies

The stability of the relationships between the US and Europe has protected trade. But such relationships were forged within World War I and World War II, when the US fought alongside the allies against Naziism and Fascism. Though we are far removed from these events, those relationships should be fostered and strengthened. Leaders change, but the legacy of those leaders can continue to bridge associations over time. We must renew our exchanges of various sorts with our allies to let them know that we are there for them, as we also hope that they will be there for us. The presumption that the US will not meet difficulties is foolhardy. Instead, we should foster these relationships in particular, so that we do not lose ground with our allies.

Middle Eastern Relationships

The US' relationship with Israel complicates its relationship with other Arab nations, given the complex situation that exists between Israel and the Palestinians. The US has, nonetheless, maintained relationships with Arab countries for many years. Despite the difficulties in the Middle East, the US ought not to disassociate itself from these other relationships despite the present difficulties.

Asian Relationships

India is poised to offer the world at large a huge number of markets. But it lacks infrastructure. The US could partner with Indian businesses to develop infrastructure for further development. The 500 million people who will become India's middle class can help to foster growth both here and there.

Taiwan

China wants Taiwan back, as President Xi made clear to President Biden in a recent meeting between the two leaders, as related on *NBC Evening News*.[25] China has scheduled return of territory, such as Hong Kong, or property, like the Chinese pandas. Taiwan is different, however, since it is a sovereign nation. Yet, its proximity to China places it in a vulnerable situation. Taiwan is a strategic trade partner with the US, given its advances in chip development, where it is generations ahead of the US and other countries. Such a strategic position places the US-Taiwan relationship in a delicate state. War is never the first order of interaction between nations. However, the US must weigh the value of what Taiwan has as it also partners with it in providing security to maintain its sovereignty. How far such measures will go is unclear. No one wants to

---

[25] *NBCEvening News*, Dec. 21, 2023.

engage the "million-man army" of China.[26] Yet, the US must evaluate how vital Taiwan is to its own prosperity, when so many devices require the use of Taiwanese technology. The company that primarily produces the chips that America needs to run its devices has received a contract to produce a plant in the West, which could protect this vital resource. Nonetheless, there must be a wait-and-see time to discern how badly Taiwan is sought after by China and whether the US will respond should China pursue such an enterprise.

African Relationships

China and Russia currently enjoy relationships with African nations that deliver huge amounts of precious metals, especially those needed for technology. America has shied away from African development and business ventures to its detriment. Such relationships could prove lucrative in the years to come in many of the same ways that such development in Central and South America could. The US needs to make overtures to African nations, so that they can be of mutual benefit.

Conclusion

Relationships can be maintained or otherwise permitted to dissolve over time. But they can also be fostered and strengthened. Fostering relationships requires the investment of resources into them and not permitting them to be ignored. Foreign relations attempt to maintain relationships between the US and other countries, so that they become stronger over time, helping each party to benefit from the relationship. This is not easily done; however, the point of our discussion was in general to appreciate that ignoring this important aspect can have far-reaching and even devastating results over time. "An ounce of prevention beats a pound of cure" is the sense that taking measures now can improve future outcomes. This is not always the case, but it seems applicable in relation to immigration. This, however, was only one issue that we attempted to examine that may seem like an area that does not involve rank-and-file Americans, but, when considered fully, must also implicate domestic

[26] Several news sources have revealed the military's inability to reach its recruitment goals. This seems disconcerting, given its recurrence.

policy. Thus, American policy, both foreign and domestic, can have significant implications for people at home, not just abroad.

Our discussion has not been exhaustive, but only illustrative. This was because the issues that involve relationships are so complex and far-reaching. Nonetheless, we ought to foster relationships with others, not undermine them. In this way, we will have more “friends” on our side, so that, should we get into trouble, we can count on others to assist us and support us. People help others more readily when they have been helped in the past. We ought not to forget such a simple gesture. If we do forget, it will be at our own peril.

The next chapter will deal with the sense of what the good is both at the individual and collective levels, since both of these aspects play into how people interact with one another, stemming from what they contend is important for realizing their own good.

8 ARE YOU GOOD?

During the Christmas season, one song indicates that Santa Claus seems to be all-knowing, recognizing when children are "naughty or nice." Children are told this fact presumably to have them change problematic behaviors, at least until Christmas time. I suppose things go back to a typical state after Christmas comes and goes. But the question of whether a person is "good" is not an easy one to answer. What is meant by good? Who established the criteria? Are the criteria related to an individual, a collective, or a combination of both? I would suggest that most people would identify themselves as good, but, here again, what does this even mean? As we endeavor to make our way toward Christmas, which is a milestone in the year, given that most people do not work that day apart from first-responders and healthcare workers, it seems appropriate to examine the sense of good that may be operative within people's lives, because different people have varying views. Otherwise, we wouldn't have such conflicts within our borders as a nation, as well as throughout the world, where people are divided in particular about the Israel-Hamas War.

Free Speech

Several presidents of leading and prestigious universities were recently called to Capitol Hill to discuss the activities that had taken place on their respective campuses. The members of Congress were appalled by the protests that took place related to the Israel-Hamas War, where some students even called for the genocide of the Jews. The presidents' permissions to engage even in this level of free speech brought about negative responses from some members of Congress, calling upon the presidents to resign or otherwise calling upon their respective colleges to fire them. In light of *another* country's war, the question is how far free speech can be permitted to go in this country.

One college president indicated that the point of no return for free speech was when conduct was implicated, that is, when students engaged in violence due to the positions that they held. There is otherwise no clear-cut answer with regard to free speech, though some on both sides have vested interests in the response. Nonetheless, the term "vested" means that people benefit from whether the response goes in one direction or the other.

But this point of contention exposes the seams of our *Constitution*, since it is being pushed to its limits. Both sides wish to appeal to the American people and others for support. Siding with either one means lending support to a specific point of view. Condoning free speech, however, ensures that dictatorial rule is not in play, but neither does one side dominate another. That is the contentious nature of this debate. Members of Congress are attempting to paint the presidents of the universities as "playing" to a side. This is not necessarily the case. Their ouster or capitulation by resigning would signal that they have caved to the pressure of influence, our law-makers. But what's the good, since this is what we have endeavored to discover, even within such a fractious situation?

The Good

The good is that which is best for the most parties concerned, at least to some extent, from an objective viewpoint. How can someone remain sufficiently distant from the events that are playing out in order to see the events from an objective vantage point even to recognize the good?

It is easy to vilify or otherwise demonize others when they reflect a different viewpoint, but describing other people in negative terms does not necessarily mean that they are bad or evil, though political and other ads engage in the practice all the time. Nor does it mean that the people doing the finger-pointing are necessarily good themselves. It merely means that some parties are attempting to control the narrative in order to ensure that a specific message is being shared. This is propaganda. But getting to the good is a different inquiry altogether. But we still need to delve into matters more to negotiate the waters, which are deep and often churn so strongly that we could drown.

The Common Good

If we move out of concern for the collective and instead focus on the individual, then I think that we can appreciate more readily what the good is, as we then branch out in other directions, namely toward understanding a collective good.

Some people might be accused of selfishness for various things that they do. However, selfishness can and must have a positive sense, at least to some extent. I must be selfish enough to eat every day and get my allotment of sleep. There are aspects of our lives that ensure that we survive, and then there are those things that take us into the realms of fulfillment and thriving. (See Maslow's "Hierarchy of Needs" described above.) If we have the resources, which should be understood in both personal and other ways, not exclusively financial, then we can realize some level of good in our lives, which is tending toward the nature of fulfillment. Some people call this happiness, though I prefer the term fulfillment. Everyone is different in this regard, as I related earlier.

We must recognize that some do not have enough of this world's goods to accommodate even their most basic needs. We recognize that there are those who have far more than plenty. It seems that there is a broad spectrum that accommodates both people's basic needs, but also time for leisure that can give rise to fulfillment, however this comes about. This is what I am referring to as "the good." This can be understood on an individual basis, because it is diverse.

But when we start extrapolating about what constitutes "the common good," we are attempting to capture a sense that involves the basic necessities of life, but also, at least to some degree, what would "fulfill" people as well. Apart from the basics, it is a difficult task to identify what will fulfill everyone, though some try to do so. Instead, we are left with a disconnect between the individual's sense of fulfillment or the individual good, and the group's or collective's sense of the same.

When we attempt to identify conduct in particular as problematic, I think it is easier to recognize certain actions that undermine others' happiness. I'm not sure that anyone would disagree that active shooter situations are detrimental to everyone except for the shooter. But when it comes to "taking sides" in relation to the conflict between Israel and Hamas, it is a different story. Whose sense of "the good" are we drawing from? This is far from clear.

The Sense of the Good

Hamas fighters attacked Israelis within Israel's own borders. Israel has every right to defend itself. But the means that Israel is using seem excessive and extreme. Yet, if they do not eradicate the power centers of Hamas within Gaza, then Israel could be attacked again.

Palestinians are being displaced by the war, moving south for safety, though even the south is now under attack. The Palestinians voted to put Hamas into power in Gaza, so their support for their government's actions has opened the door to their grave destruction. But they have been treated badly by the Israelis for years, especially with a walled-in existence that subjects people to random searches and treatment that has consistently been problematic, as even some Jews admit.

The acrimony has now come to a head. But where is the collective good? The problem is which collective we are speaking about.

Collective Good

During war-time, I doubt if anyone recognizes much fulfillment. Yet, how much are others' problems our own? No one can answer this point, but it will determine how readily a person implicates him or herself in the actions of others.

When people attend a sports event or a concert, they may "live vicariously" through the event itself. This is possible. It may even be visceral for them. Some people sometimes don "strange" outfits to underscore how much they identify with the event or team or something else. The same is true with how we identify with other nations, which, in a "melting pot" like America, will have many individuals who identify with those who are engaged in the struggle in Gaza. Is it because of a similar heritage? Is it due to one's sense of humanity? Is it due to one's ethnicity? Who can say? However, the recognition for why people involve themselves may obfuscate the sense of the good that all of us should be aspiring to. Are we allying ourselves with others, not because we love them, but because we hate the other people whom they are fighting? This, it seems to me, is poignant for discerning the good. Are we engaging in our activity that demonstrates support out of a positive sense of working toward the positive good of the other, or are we undermining the other simply to effect negativity on them? These points are not the same. Whose good are we looking to support? Are we truly working toward such an endeavor?

Fulfillment Revisited

Everyone wants the same thing from my perspective, it may simply be realized in different ways. But do I have to exclude one person's sense of fulfillment over another's? Sometimes this must take place. But it is a difficult point to impose one's collective sense of the good on others. In this country at least, multiple senses of the good at the collective level must co-exist, which is what our Founders developed for us. It may not make for the most harmonious encounters, but the ability to consider such matters in the public forum underscores how valuable this society that we have built over time is that we often take for granted. People wish to advocate for their own sense of how to make the world a better place. Our society permits differing understandings of the good in order to realize such ideals. There is a commonality among us in relation to the pursuit of happiness that all of us attempt, yet each of us is different in that pursuit. We leave it to our legislature to ensure protections under the law, so that people can lead their lives in relative safety and security. It is important, however, to realize that the law cannot always promote "the good" of collectives. Instead, it attempts to protect groups from incursions by others. We are fortunate to have such protections in place.

But living out of a protectionist perspective is far from thriving. We need to engage with each other, so that we recognize the varied views that can help to stir new insights. Dartmouth College attempted to bring this about by discussion sessions among thousands of students. This seems to be an astute model to follow. The shame of it all is that the presidents of other prestigious universities did not engage in this practice, which placed them under fire—they have now all resigned. Had they engaged their students in such a way, members of Congress would probably not have been so acrimonious. Once again, there are lessons to be learned for all parties in these matters. The question is whether anyone will learn them and implement their implications.

Conclusion

When looking at whose naughty or nice, we may tend to lose track that people want some sense of fulfillment in their lives. Nonetheless, it can only be when we appreciate the individual good toward which we aspire that we can then evaluate the collective goods that others offer to us, though some may tend to reverse this process. Both options exist. We must recognize how such goods fit within a vast panoply of other people's goods. This is not an easy task. Nonetheless, by appreciating what America is, we can see that even acrimony can serve as a means of learning. It may not be easy to take, but through listening and discussion, we can come to appreciate others' perspectives. When we do so, we, too, can recognize what our society was meant to be. Our Founders have placed directives to guide us in our exchanges with others. Let's be clear about what they offer to us, as we continue to delve into what will drive us to a deeper sense of fulfillment.

The next chapter considers the limits of free speech as it also recognizes recent situations that have pushed this Constitutional sense to its limits.

9 LIMITS TO FREE SPEECH

We have examined free speech in general as a right granted by *the Constitution*, but free speech, like anything else, must have limits or else it can devolve into "hate" speech or speech so provocative that it fosters violence by its subject matter and other contributing factors. Though it is difficult to appeal to leaders or leadership, in general, such appeals must also be expressed, since they also play a role. Our discussion, then, will attempt to appreciate how speech can be limited in some circumstances for a variety of reasons.

Yelling "Fire"

To yell "fire" in a crowded movie theatre or elsewhere when there is no fire is an exercise of free speech, since it demonstrates how anyone can say anything that he or she wishes. However, when such statements will bring about harm to others through unnecessary agitation toward an emergency situation, then, as the Supreme Court has ruled, engagement in such an action constitutes a willful act toward causing pain to others. Such exercise of free speech is not protected under the First Amendment.

Inciting Violence

Neither is it appropriate for people to incite others to violence. If words are used to propel people to violence, then they represent a boundary beyond which people ought not go, but they themselves are working toward undermining the common good of some in a deliberate fashion.

Such deliberate acts, even when limited to speech, can be construed as problematic. Is it, then, an exercise in free speech to permit people to call for the eradication of the Jewish people during a protest? Or of any others? If the call were to engage a group in this country for purposes of inciting violence, then even the instigators could be held culpable. If they are inciting acts outside of the borders of the US, then the matters seem to take on a different pallor. Nonetheless, encouraging violence in some form offers a conundrum for discerning the limits of free speech, especially within a time and environment that has a negative transcendence that leads unquestionably in such a direction.

Riots and Violence

We should appreciate that protests can become violent, especially if there is no one or nothing to rein people in, depending on the matter at hand. In light of protests' escalation into violence, law enforcement has every right to quell violence where it breaks out, given that such circumstances can easily escalate into mayhem leading to the destruction of property and violence against persons. This has occurred in various locations throughout the country, where law enforcement was too late or otherwise recognized that the violence that protestors were engaged in was too much for their forces to contain. Peaceful protest thus can devolve into violent mayhem in short order, depending on the situation and circumstances. Law enforcement must decide what should be done given their proximity to the area in question. Those who engage in violence must pay the price for their unwillingness to control themselves, though oftentimes they are the area businesses that sadly pay the price for others' unwillingness to do so. Law enforcement has every reason to take definitive and decisive action to quell such unrest.

Leadership

We spoke earlier of the general populace encouraging violence; however, when leadership engages in the practice of inciting violence, then leaders are also culpable. We tend toward holding only individuals accountable in such circumstances, which is appropriate, given that people engage in specific conduct that may be adjudicated under the law. However, we tend not to give credence to understanding that leaders also can encourage wrong-doing, either tacitly or overtly. The movie, *A Few Good Men* (1992), describes how a Marine colonel is willing to order a disciplinary tactic against one of his own men to "get him into shape."[27] Sadly, the Marine dies as a result of the disciplinary action. This causes an investigation, which ultimately undercovers the commanding officer's wrong-doing. It is difficult to trace back the "order," but the "chain of command" within the military is clear. Leadership, then, can be implicated in wrong-doing that it orders, though the process of uncovering such orders may be arduous.

Military Free Speech

I am not familiar with military law, but I would contend that there must be limits placed on free speech within the military, given that the morale of troops is involved. The military are in a unique position to defend the ends of the US government. These are articulated through the chain of command. Soldiers may disagree with policy decisions, but they must comply with them, given the nature of the military as a top-down system of governance in its own right that follows such a vehicle of information exchange. Members of the military, then, must curtail their public expression of free speech, which may involve haircuts, display of tattoos and other overt expression, so that morale may be maintained.

It is my experience that some colleges and universities discourage careers in the service and even discourage certain government agencies from recruiting on their campuses. I cannot know the rationale behind the exclusion, only that the process of exclusion does exist. Colleges and universities may see such curtailment of rights as described above as a direct attack against them and their values. Despite this, there must be a coherent understanding of the reason behind the military. It may not be the place for the freest expression, but it does serve as the prime protector for the rights found in *the Constitution*, though those same rights may not be as demonstrable within its ranks as they may be in other areas of American life. This is part of the price of living within a pluralistic society like our

---

[27] *A Few Good Men*. Directed by Rob Reiner. Columbia Pictures. 1992. https://en.wikipedia.org/wiki/A_Few_Good_Men. Last edited 7 March 2024

own.

Hate Speech

Hate speech, where people bring others down through the language that they use or who otherwise foment hatred, seems ancillary in that, unless such speech leads to violence, it may or not be taken into account. There is a boundary that some people cross that leads them into the realm of violence, but this is not always the case, which makes such cases difficult. The mere expression of hatred toward others is not necessarily culpable behavior, apart from the cases above, but it can be brought to demonstrate intent if actions become violent. This places a great burden on law enforcement given the line that they must straddle. Our country in general has tread this line lightly. The freedom of speech that we enjoy must take into account that some will not be able to "hold this line" and will instead cross it. This is an unfortunate consequence of free speech as well.

Conclusion

Freedom of speech is enshrined within the First Amendment to *the Constitution*, but its purpose is to ensure that government acts uprightly, so that it does not impose itself on the citizenry. However, when rank and file people attempt to incite violence or otherwise make false claims, then those claims must be evaluated for their ability to harm others. We examined several instances where free speech ought to be limited given the level of harm that could occur. We also looked at military understandings, where expression may be limited for a specific purpose. This follows in that morale must be maintained among those who protect the integrity of the laws of the land. It seems like a double standard, but I believe that it exists for a purpose and such a label is not without merit.

There are, then, different trajectories within the same nation; this seems evident. But equally evident is that the nation clarifies boundaries through and by the expression of free speech. In dealing with cases that "push the envelope," our judicial system is able to contend with what constitutes violations, so that people can more readily appreciate a clearer path. The path is not always straight or clear, but no document can articulate all circumstances. Instead, our Founders left us with statements that are sufficiently flexible to withstand the ebbs and flows of time and their consequences toward change. All must be open to change. Dynamism is the nature of life. With no dynamism or change, there can be no life. Discerning what fosters or undermines our lives is the nature of what free speech is about.

Free speech and its limits can help to identify boundaries that are in place to protect, but also limit people. The next chapter deals with some social issues where people hold sometimes contentious positions. We should not shy away from discussing these positions.

10 SOME SOCIAL ISSUES

Trust is the pre-cursor that makes any sort of dialogue possible, given that it serves as a bridge of sorts that can connect people together. When trust is in play, people are ready listen, but also engage in the process of attempting to understand where others are coming from. Engagement with others does not mean agreement with their positions. Nonetheless, its presence, which often goes unnoticed, manifests itself in a manner that can often be elusive, but it is nonetheless there. It is often indescribable. In fact, its enactment can often only be recognized ex post facto, that is, in hindsight. When there is no trust, substantive dialogue is not possible. However, when it is present, new horizons can manifest themselves, which can bring about new beginnings, new creations, in how people view various issues.

The following paragraphs will address hot-button topics deliberately with an eye to appreciating how trust can deliver new insight into areas that oftentimes reflect "sacred" or "untouchable" formulations. But, as with many sacred workings, going further into them can reveal further depth. If we are afraid of such plumbs into the depths, then we are afraid of deepening our perspectives. Some may fight such inquiries. I can appreciate such reluctance. Nonetheless, I believe that the discussions below will serve to highlight where further discussion can bring new-found wisdom, so that we can move forward in our country, but also reflect the manner in which we live our lives.

Guns and Gun Violence

There is no escaping the sadly ubiquitous nature of gun violence in our society. There is also no escaping that the Second Amendment enshrines the ability of the citizens of our country to bear arms. I must state that I worked at Smith & Wesson for six months when it was headquartered in Springfield, Massachusetts, functioning as a temporary secretary there. I found one individual in particular zealous about guns in the way in which he invited me to go shooting with him. I took him up on his kind invitation, as I have with others during my life. I do not own a gun, but I can appreciate that some individuals enjoy the pastime of shooting for sport, be that hunting or target practice or some other activity. Smith & Wesson has been targeted for its part to play in producing weaponry. I cannot comment on this point. However, I can comment on the zeal that my co-worker had in shooting to such an extent that he invited me to join him in a favorite endeavor of his. Zeal is the hook that people bring from within themselves, which is "something" that can draw others to join them. Shooting can be a simple form of recreation for some. I sensed the zeal of the individual who invited me to join him.

But some have taken their right to bear arms to an extreme level, which is something more than simply zeal. This can point to extremism. I can appreciate that there are some who become extreme, because they fear that their right to bear arms may be rescinded. This is a difficult circumstance for them. Such a threat can make people paranoid to such an extent that they become hyper-vigilant, which, in turn, leads to further fixation on guns and the inability to recognize reasonable approaches to addressing gun violence. There can be no doubt that limiting some people's ability to purchase guns and limiting the availability of certain types of weaponry is in the interests of the country. No manufacturer should be producing mechanisms that can turn a rifle into an automatic weapon, so that rank-and-file individuals have access to these weapons, which can be particularly destructive. Limitations, then, on people's rights to own certain types of weapons or mandating background checks is not against *the Constitution*. People should have the right to purchase firearms, but not all firearms should be available for purchase.

Additionally, children should not be using firearms outside the supervision of parents or guardians. Most states require children to drive with a licensed driver while holding a driver's permit for some period. Why would we not have similar requirements to protect the general public from underage gun users? Limitations for adults is of a different nature, since it is difficult to evaluate people for mental illness or similar difficulties, which can contribute to gun violence. This remains an area for discussion.

Many vocal opponents toward limitations of guns of any kind might express their chagrin for such measures. But a discussion into this arena must involve why people use and have firearms. In many circumstances, people want to protect themselves. This, however, begs the question about why they cannot rely upon law enforcement in their areas to carry out such an enterprise. Is there a paranoia about other people encroaching upon their land or other domain? In such a discussion, people could discern whether a fear stems from a mental illness, an earlier difficulty in life producing such a reaction, or something else. Nonetheless, discussion must broach such topics lightly, because zeal for a pastime can become confused with paranoia over the loss of this Constitutional right. Limitations can co-exist with Constitutional rights, but are we willing to examine them with a view to trust rather than "getting our way"?

Such an approach will pervade all of the discussions below in one fashion or another. What is the public good versus what does the individual want? Such a sliding scale is always problematic. There are no simple solutions to these complex problems. Discussion helps to hammer out the details of what stands in the way of agreement, which often sees both (or more) sides losing in some ways, but also both sides gaining in some ways, especially in relation to the common good.

Active Shooters

Active shooters, most of whom are (young) males, engage in wanton destruction for a variety of reasons. The actions of these individuals are most unfortunate, but I do not believe that banning weapons of every kind will address the issues that lead to individuals who manifest "perfect storms" of rage, so that they kill innocent people, especially children and typically ethnic minorities. These men were typically treated with derision and disrespect throughout their lives. They had no way of dealing with the depth of their rage, which never dissipated, so they became active shooters. The process seems typical in scope to PTSD. These individuals typically have death wishes, which is oftentimes realized due to their actions. Antibullying measures in schools need to recognize how students isolate other students when they can. Teachers can intervene when they see such incidents occur, but they must also be caring enough to assist such individuals with recognizing caring and compassion. This, it seems to me, is the only way to offset this level of rage, that is, to deal with it early and offer helps for realizing compassion and self-worth.

Healthcare

Insurance in general involves taking premiums from individuals who sign up for a benefit of some sort, then contribute their money toward a pool of resources that delivers back to them should they need the benefit, for instance, life insurance, home-owner's insurance, car insurance, and the like. This same model applies to Social Security and Medicare programs, run by the government, but it also involves the national education program, since those who have special needs may require expenditures that are offset by the collected resources from those who have no such need. The question must always be asked whether the number of participants within any program can support the outlays. In California and Florida, insurance premiums are high or insurance companies have left those states altogether, because the amount of resources being paid out from the insurance pool has overwhelmed the amount that comes from people's premiums. In light of extreme weather and destruction from these events, there isn't enough money for insurance companies to make a profit, which can force them out of business. This is the perpetual dilemma stemming from all such group programs.

Healthcare is similar, yet it involves people's lives. People like to contend that life's value is infinite, but no one can live this way. There must be limits, because resources, like everything else, are limited. When we work together to build systems that accommodate people's health issues, there must be give and take. Medicare offers a socialized methodology for dealing with a broad population's health concerns. It is imperfect; however, it is the system that we have. Many physicians and other healthcare practitioners balk at its payments and even elect not to treat people who have only Medicare as their insurance.

Physicians wish to capitalize on their years of education and sacrifice by earning a higher income. There is nothing wrong with this. However, I would suggest that they and other highly paid professions, such as attorneys, though others as well, must always give back to society through some pro bono work or otherwise serving the indigent in some manner (four hours per month?). I believe that anyone in a position that gains from society should also give back to it. Some may disagree. Nonetheless, we are in a crisis within healthcare across the board. There are too few primary care physicians, nurses, and people in other fields. People want to make a decent wage to be sure, but unless we examine healthcare from all angles, then we will not be able properly to address such concerns, where equity across all fronts is addressed. All people value their health. Like education, healthcare is currently contending with too many variables, especially the human ones. We need to examine all facets in earnest or we risk a catastrophe.

Wellness Initiatives

I am in good health and endeavor to remain that way by watching my diet, exercising, and annual visits to a physician to check out my current health status. I am not overly cautious about such things, though I believe that my concerns have become heightened as I have gotten older. I attempt to take reasonable steps to overcome high cholesterol and some age-related aches and pains. I typically follow my physician's advice. I believe that I am doing everything that I can to maintain good physical and emotional health. Addressing difficulties in their early stages can save me and others from more invasive procedures and treatments later on. Part of the maintenance of one's health can involve taking prescription medication.

Prescription Medication

Many people take prescription medication, especially the elderly. Without the help of insurance, such costs can be overwhelming, which I have found in my own life. Keeping prescription costs down is an important step in cutting overall healthcare costs. On the one hand, pharmaceutical firms expend enormous resources in bringing drugs to market. America maintains some of the safest protocols in the world for demonstrating drug effectiveness and safety. Such protocols require time and resources to implement and maintain. Pharmaceuticals have the right to regain their investment expended in research and development. On the other hand, the government and major insurance carriers have the ability to obtain significant discounts from vendors for them to discount drug prices, especially generic drugs. Generic drugs should be the prescription of choice where possible. Some stand in the way of such cost-cutting measures. These hurdles must be overcome.

Pre-existing Conditions

My understanding is that there are about fifteen or so health conditions that affect the majority of people, such as diabetes and heart disease. Most people who have these conditions have only one, but there is a significant minority who also have multiple conditions to contend with. The purpose of the Healthcare Marketplace within states is to provide low-cost health insurance, which means that the more people who contribute to it through their premiums, the more people can be covered in general. Insurance companies must limit some services; this is true. Premiums must increase for those who seek more services. This is the nature of such a plan, which I believe attempts to be equitable. A marketplace permits people to evaluate their needs in light of the services offered. I believe, however, that insurance companies need to do a better job at identifying what they cover in easy-to-read ways, so that people know what they are buying into and what those services are. This is not always the case, as I presented earlier.

Catastrophic Healthcare Insurance

People can suddenly become sick even though they have lived healthy lifestyles and even when they have watched their health throughout their lives. Nonetheless, healthcare costs are such that people can lose their resources at an alarming rate should a health crisis arise. Catastrophic health insurance should be available to people so as to preserve their resources. I have heard of "reverse life insurance" and other similar options in relation to long-term care options. I believe that such options are crucial, so that people can preserve their holdings in the midst of ever-sky-rocketing healthcare costs.

Abortion Rights

I admit that I am pro-life; God is the source of all life. So, I invite scrutiny of my comments, given that I have a recognized bias. Nonetheless, I can appreciate that some view life as a sliding scale related to a fetus' development in the womb. As a fetus develops, it may become more "human" over time and thus more valuable, so that some tend to view earlier term abortions as permissible under their ethical guidelines, whereas later term abortions may cause difficulty for most. Some contend that human life begins with conception and therefore ought to be protected at all stages of development. This is where I identify myself.

Some have views that may include those detailed above, but may be even further nuanced. When a fetus has a genetically determinable disease, which is terminal, then they may contend that the parents should have the ability to abort such a child. If the mother's life is in danger or if conception occurs due to rape or incest, then, once again, the mother should be able to procure an abortion to address such difficult circumstances. There is room for discussion and understanding in all of these arenas.

However, I find a general lack of opportunity for discussion when women claim a "right" to an abortion for whatever reason. My difficulty stems largely from viewing this medical procedure as akin to every other. I would suggest that it is different explicitly because it involves human life. Additionally, I have linked it with a discussion about gun violence, because I view abortion as violence perpetrated against the unborn. Violence of any kind is problematic. Abortion as a violent act is seldom articulated. We will discuss aggression below, but I believe that this point resonates here as well.

When people claim that women should have "reproductive rights," that is, the ability to protect against pregnancy, then I believe that they must follow their consciences. But I wonder why the women involved in such cases did not consider the consequences of their actions prior to engagement in sexual intercourse in the first place. I have read pieces in newspapers where some women use abortion as a method of birth control. I find the practice abhorrent, and it makes me wonder why responsibility and accountability do not function in discussions related to reproductive rights. The ability to engage in sexual activity is part of what it means to be human. But a deliberate unwillingness to avoid pregnancy through natural family planning (NFP) or contraception of some variety seems problematic. When someone flagrantly embraces such a practice as abortion is, I would suggest that it serves to undermine the cause to preserve abortion in the exceptional cases as delimited above. The suggestion that abortion should be kept legal to permit reckless behavior is more than problematic. We should also appreciate that two parties must always be involved in engagement in sexual intercourse. In no way should people conclude that decisions are solely in the hands of women at such a time. Men are as responsible for such circumstances. Accountability is appropriate and necessary for all people involved.

Roe v. Wade

Having made such an argument, however, I can appreciate that the statute guiding the law of the land for 49 years has been *Roe v. Wade* (1973).[28] The suggestion that, with the stroke of a pen, a cultural narrative about abortion can be changed overnight is absurd. I am aware of condemnatory narratives related to replacing *Roe v. Wade*, but I am aware of only a few articulations related to life. These are also necessary and in need of equal time. Appreciating life as precious is one such narrative, but so is the appeal to women to view motherhood in a positive light. The ability to procure an abortion so easily, even on a whim, suggests that having children can upset one's life solely in a negative manner. This *can and probably will* occur. But having one's life upended by children can also lead to a rewarding experience. Control of every circumstance is not the only way to fulfillment. Admittedly, I have no children of my own, but from my discussions with others, which have-been many, people can and do find meaning in having and rearing children, even, if not especially, children with disabilities, who require a different level of care and concern. A discussion about how people gain meaning in their lives beyond making

---

[28] Supreme Court, *Roe v. Wade*, 1973. https://supreme.justia.com/cases/federal/us/410/113/.

a living and the like can help people to recognize the multifaceted nature of what caring for others can bring to people's lives. I am not condemning the practice of abortion as much as wondering if people have considered the positive impact that having a child can have.

Contraception

Some of the rhetoric flowing from the "far right" instills paranoia in women and others that safe methods of contraception may be removed from availability. Such practices can serve to force people to "dig in their heals" about abortion rights even more, as was already discussed in relation to guns. A discussion about safe and responsible options of contraception must take place, as they must also be kept legal and available, otherwise the long-standing implications of abortion will continue to persevere, when this is no longer the universal law of the land. The law, however, has changed in some places; however, the attitude that underlies such a position is also in need of revision. I maintain that there is a distinction between abortion and abortifacients on the one hand and contraception on the other, keeping with my comments above. Though I believe that people ought to have the availability of contraceptives according to their consciences, employers, owing to their consciences as well, should have the right *not* to pay for contraceptives or anything else that does not fit within their belief systems. There should be no mandate that undermines conscience rights for anyone.[29]

[29] The 8th Circuit Court of Appeals recently struck down an appeal by the Biden Administration to require physicians to perform sex re-assignment surgery, even against their consciences, and to require financial support through insurance. See "Like 5th Circuit, 8th Circuit Strikes Down Biden's Transgender Mandate," *The Pilot*, 20 December 22. https://www.thebostonpilot.com/article.php?ID=193779. Physicians should not be compelled to go against their consciences in performing these surgeries or abortions. See also Samuel Lovett, "Tavistock Gender Clinic Facing Legal Action Over 'Failure of Care' Claims," *The Independent*, 11 August 2022. https://www.independent.co.uk/news/health/tavistock-gender-clinic-lawyers-latest-b2143006.html.

In Sum

The comments above detail healthcare concerns, since I believe that they affect most people in poignant ways. The issues that follow affect fewer and fewer populations, but they are nonetheless important. I do not treat them, however, in as much detail.

Women's Rights

Women have been slighted in their quest for equal rights in society, such as equal pay for equal work. I do not believe that aborting children is an appropriate path toward realizing equality within society. Making the innocent pay for advancement may be the way of the world, but it is not a moral or ethical practice that I endorse. Instead, most people can appreciate hard work as the basis upon which most advance. Paths to such advancement may need re-examination in the lives of women, especially when women work differently from men. I have found that women are more collaborative, whereas men work independently more often. Nonetheless, such differences in work practice should still lead to ways in which people can advance within companies and other venues. Discussing such differences need not lead to impasses, but instead understanding so as to make progress.

Gay Rights

Gay rights are the law of the land. Religious people should not seek to undermine these rights, nor should homosexuals seek to defame the sensibilities of religious people. Both groups can live in harmony. Conservative legislatures have sadly attempted to undermine gay rights through underhanded methods, some of which have been rightly deemed unconstitutional. Such efforts underscore how some work to destroy others rather than discuss matters with them, so that both groups can work toward mutual understanding. There is need for further discussion, especially between and among conservative groups and those who identify as homosexual.

Trans-sexualism

I have to admit to my own questions about transsexualism. These individuals have their own difficulties to contend with. Nonetheless, I have trouble with how they are "singled out" for special accommodation beyond any other group, even to the point of changing standard English to accommodate them. I do not advocate discrimination, but neither do I advocate special status. Part of fitting into society is the ability to accept oneself and deal with people's reactions to us, not forcing others to accept us. Some of the training that I have received from various institutions and school districts tends toward treating transgender people in a manner different from others. I do not share this view. I do not hold transexuals in disrepute.

I believe that transgender people ought to be clear about what they are doing in undergoing sex reassignment surgery. Given the extremely invasive nature of such treatments and procedures, seeking this type of surgery needs to be in consultation with mental health practitioners, but also only conducted with permission of parents when individuals are under the age of 18.[30]

Law and Society

Laws can have an effect on the citizenry, so that people adopt the practices identified within those laws, which can cause social unrest and fissures, but, over time, can also bring about cohesion and healing. Our present societal direction tends toward favoring the individual over the group. This can undermine how we view the police, for instance, so that people do not

---

[30] There is litigation across the country relating to schools using students' "preferred pronouns" during school hours, whereas parents are not informed about their children's decisions to engage in such practices. Schools have moved in the direction of protecting student academic and other information at the level of Health Insurance Portability and Accountability Act (HIPAA; 1996) regulations, which relates to the confidentiality of medical information. The "Every Student Succeeds Act" (2015) does lean in this direction; however, the practice followed by schools seems a clear violation of the foundational relationship between parents/guardians and children, which undergirds the importance of the family within society. Within the scope of HIPAA, people could lose their jobs or health insurance should others learn of a diagnosis or a pre-existent condition, for example, AIDS or diabetes. This is not the case for children's academic or other information. There is a need for the Supreme Court or another court to re-examine the level of privacy and protections that are due to minors over their parents or legal guardians. Additionally, the place and scope of confidentially in relation to "school counselors" must also be evaluated, given the role that they now take within schools, which can often obfuscate the authority of principals.

undertake this important profession. Even our schools tend toward such an emphasis on the individual to the detriment of societal achievement and standards. Our current economic troubles also play into such an understanding. Government or collectives can help to rein in too much individualism through laws, but such laws will only be effective to the extent that people trust in law enforcement and "buy into" the purpose behind the laws and practices themselves. When people view laws as oppressive or attempting to keep people down or otherwise hamper rights, then they will not inculcate them in a real fashion into their lives. Such laws are, then, ineffective. The general sense of not stealing comes to mind in relation to the "smash and grabs" that have recently been occurring throughout the country. The individual's notion of right and wrong is overriding the general sense of protection of property. Too much of these actions will lead to copy-cats, but also the continued dismantling of collective understandings of culture in general, and right and wrong in particular. There is a balance that must be maintained, which is currently eroding. Laws, enforcement, consistency, as well as trust, must be realized or we will see a further devolution occur in our society.

Conclusion

I have sought to appreciate how trust's presence, which is oftentimes elusive, must obtain or else discussion can fall flat. Instead, when people recognize the engagement of others and their willingness to listen, more than just hear, others' concerns, then we can make headway. If, instead, we do not recognize those whose views may have turned extreme through paranoia, then bringing people into dialogue will not occur. By enunciating at least some issues, both their pros and cons, if only from my own or others' biased attitudes, I believe that further discussion can help to appreciate the multifaceted nature of issues more clearly. Clarity of expression can help to uncover wisdom for approaches that lead to progress in general. We are in need of new ways to progress in most areas of our country. Discussions, when undertaken in engaging ways, can lead to realizing such progress, but only when people are willing to recognize new ways of looking at things, which oftentimes involves listening to others to gain their perspectives, but this can only happen when trust is in evidence.

The next chapter will delve into individual rights to work in tandem with collective rights, which were detailed earlier. The ability to work together in transcendence is an important aspect of working out clear-cut goals.

11 RIGHTS AND THE INDIVIDUAL

I hear a lot about rights on television, that is, people demanding equal rights in this way or that. When people feel "stepped on," then they can wonder whether it is a manifestation of a concerted effort to undermine their Constitutional or other rights. Everyone has a right to such a concern, and it is often warranted, though not always. Some may attempt to commandeer movements in order to advance their own cause(s), which, when evaluated from a wider view, has nothing to do with the matter at hand. They align themselves to ride the wave, so to speak, which can advance themselves due to others' hard work. But this is dishonest. Instead, as I have identified earlier, people need to take stock in their own lives and circumstances, but this can also come from a sense of transcendence, where the whole is greater than the sum of the parts. By this I mean that individuals must recognize their own innate value, which comes from dealing with sometimes disheartening and troublesome events. If people do not do this, then I believe that they will be easy fodder for charlatans, but also authoritarian notions that promise great things, but, when pressed, will ultimately deliver misery and confusion to most. I believe that this is due to a false notion of individualism, which has taken hold in our country, where collective concerns are viewed as the enemy. I would suggest that merging both a sober sense of individualism with the place of the collective can achieve great things, especially transcendence, which can assist us in working toward a more positive future for everyone.

Authoritarianism

More regimes than not across the globe are authoritarian, that is, dictatorships. The rise of such regimes, even in the West, should be something that all of us not only recognize, but also appreciate as part of the landscape that will attempt to make gains even within this country. For the past several decades, since at least the Vietnam era, as a nation we have experienced culture wars. I can only suggest that they represent the clash between laissez-faire understandings and those that have viewed collectivist understandings as sacrosanct. The backlash against collectivist understandings has been dramatic, especially in recent times. This can be seen as a good thing in some ways, since it has yielded recognition of the need for civil rights of all kinds, most notably for the disabled, women, minority populations, and many others. However, my concern is for the individuated self, more than it is for any class or group. How does the individual fare in light of the current climate that all of us experience?

Freedom

People want to be free, but all freedom is limited and circumscribed. No one person can do anything that he or she pleases. The image of people in their cars getting from one location to their destination is an apt metaphor, as related above. But we must also be skilled drivers in our own right. The flow of traffic can take us in certain directions, but such detours are typically exceptional, not the norm. And following trajectories that others identify for us remains one of my concerns, especially in relation to authoritarianism, but also in terms of bullying by any persons or groups who wish to enforce their agendas to the detriment of others' freedom to self-determination. But the other side of such a concern involves how people develop into individuals and their affinity toward collectives.

The Good of the People

I separate governmental systems in distinct ways. England has a Constitutional monarchy which has a king, but that monarch serves only honorary roles. Their parliament makes the decisions that govern their country. Other democracies in the West have similar systems of government.

But countries, such as Saudi Arabia or similar States, are run in different ways. They may have an oligarchy that governs, but they work toward the good of their people, not toward its enslavement or impoverishment. At least this is how I assess such governments across the globe. There are also oppressive states, such as North Korea, that work toward the State's supremacy in all things. This was part of the vision of Communism in general, where the collective matters, not the individual.

When it comes to the US, the hope is that our system works toward the betterment of its people. But I personally view our weakness as an inability to see the importance of the collective, especially when it comes to the development of the individual apart from the collective, but also in how the individual relates to the collective, since there are quests that must take place in earnest at the collective level, which serve to protect the freedoms that all of us enjoy, and that is in large part due to the police and military, which we have developed above.

The Military

It would be a wonderful vision not to rely on military-readiness for our country's defense. However, such a utopian view is far from our current state of affairs. Instead, with a sense of prudence, the US must maintain appropriate armed forces and other defenses that ensure the integrity of our nation's security, so that citizens can enjoy the fruits of freedom that military personnel and other civil servants maintain for them.

I have personally heard individuals wonder about the need for the military. I believe that they lack perspective in appreciating the many areas that the military must exercise its ability to deter aggression, so that others will not act against our country. I believe that a strong deterrence works to dissuade foreign threats, so the mission of the US toward its national security protects our borders (and those of our allies in certain cases), so that the US can work toward appropriate growth in delivering freedom for its citizens.

The Collective and Culture

Cultural understandings may reflect distinct perspectives and vary widely. However, our legal system, which has its basis in our founding documents, especially *the Constitution*, provides the underpinning for people's ability to work through difficulties with others. Contentions develop over time, but juris prudence can offer relief. It is an imperfect system; however, it is a necessary one. But I believe that all of the understandings presented above can benefit from appreciation of transcendence that I have only briefly mentioned. However, I believe that this sense is pivotal to any long-standing progress or achievement, but especially in the political realm.

Individuals must recognize that they are themselves more than the sum of their parts. Scientific inquiry serves to gain forensic evidence which can contribute toward our self-understanding. Advances during the Enlightenment period (17th-18th c.) brought about such "revelations." But science does not typically foster a sense of transcendence, though I believe that it is just as vital as forensic inquiry.

Transcendent Views

From individual's self-understanding, to a couple's appreciation of their interconnectedness, to teams' ability to work toward a common goal, transcendence is the "process" or the "synergy," that takes people into the realm of the unknown. It is typically an artistic attitude, I suppose, but this does not mean that it must only be realized within the artistic realm, as important as this is. Instead, the need for common goals and trajectories can help us to rely on others in ways that assist us in working toward ever greater ends that may have been elusive where only one or two attempt the endeavor. Instead, recognition of the existence of transcendence can help to bring about different ends, which may only be slightly distinct from others, yet they can more fully deliver their intended result. After all, people want to realize fulfillment in their lives. I believe that this is true of everyone, and an appropriate reading of what "the pursuit of happiness" is about as relayed in *the Constitution.* This common good is the objective of us all. Transcendence helps us to realize it, perhaps through disparate and, at times, antagonistic ways, but I believe that the willingness to work out such dilemmas is possible.

Conclusion

Authoritarianism currently accounts for more governmental systems around the world than democracies. Even some democracies have leaned in this direction in recent times. I believe that such a governmental approach is detrimental to the fabric of democracy, but also undermines people's fulfillment. But I also believe that a laissez-faire understanding, which would undermine necessary collective bodies, such as the police or the military, but others as well, can also cause problems in maintaining a balance that can assure people their ability to realize relative peace and freedom. The *authoritative* approach, as opposed to the *authoritarian* approach, which identifies consequences for actions and takes them seriously, is distinct from either of the earlier models, but I believe that it strikes a balance between these two extremes.

Balance is important, but it can also be elusive, as culture wars attempt to fight it out as though they were in the arena of ancient Rome. Instead, we ought to tap such heart-felt and powerful energy into transcendent perspectives that can help us to bridge gaps that many can agree upon. This can lead us to yet other perspectives, where people can realize freedom, happiness, and relative peace within the fabric of their lives, which are lived *with others, not in isolation from them.*

Individuals, however, need to balance their own value with their own ability to be reckless. Accepting responsibility for one's actions helps people to become mature individuals. Unless and until the majority of us do so, we shall be mired in a false sense of individualism, which makes people susceptible to authoritarianism, but also other schemes that will not lead us forward. The individual must not be afraid of the collective, but must also recognize within him or herself one's innate value. Only when the majority accomplish this will we realize progress in enduring ways both for ourselves and for our country as a whole.

The next chapter will discuss what peace is and what it is not. Peace can have different perspectives admittedly. Our discussion will attempt to hash some of these out.

12 PEACE

People have their own insights or understandings about what *peace* means or entails, which implicates how people will, in turn, appreciate what peace is. In some manner, however, it involves the cessation of forces. I use vague terms because there are at least two kinds of peace, which implicate each other. There is internal peace, which means that a person has some level of self-mastery, bringing with it an internal calm, which some refer to as *peace*. There is, of course, the other, more common sense of the term, which means that our borders are protected and battles have ceased, so that people live their lives in a state where physical skirmishes involving weaponry and the like no longer occur. We can examine both of these senses from the inside out or the outside in. I'm not sure that is matters, though I do believe that they can work in tandem. Having said this, I believe that doing two things at the same time is a particularly difficult task for anyone. Nonetheless, just because something is difficult does not mean that we should not try it. This will be how we shall proceed with our discussion of peace.

Complexities of War

As we examined the complexity for how foreign policy can implicate domestic policy and vice versa, so we can also look at the complexities involved with how wars begin. The Israel-Hamas War seems an apt place to begin, given that everyone knows about it from the news, at least this is primarily where I am getting my information.

Hamas, the governing party of Gaza and the West Bank, rules over these regions, but it has also been deemed a terrorist organization. The people of Gaza voted this party in as their leadership for what is surely another complex development over time. Hamas must have a standing "army" or at least forces to bring to bear against aggressors, since Israel, during its attack on Gaza, has attempted to distinguish Hamas fighters from the general population. Additionally, there were people who engaged in the attacks against Israel on 7 October 2023.

The people of Gaza should not be equated with their government leaders. Citizens vote their leaders in, but people may also be limited in their selections. As in our own elections here in the US, people may be selecting the person or party that will do the least damage, rather than because they endorse such a person or party. The argument that the Palestinians "chose" Hamas and are therefore culpable for their "choice" is problematic.

The US and Israel contend that Iran is operating "behind the scenes" in coordinating attacks against the US and other entities around the Suez Canal and other locales, especially from Yemen, which has been at war for years. Yemen serves as a battleground for different factions within at least two Arab states, especially Saudi Arabia and the United Arab Emirates (UAE). Again, a state or country can become the "tool" of political forces that have resources available to them, where rank and file citizens are, in effect, at their mercy.

For many years, Israel has treated Palestinians as "second-class" citizens. But what does such a moniker mean?

Second-Class Citizens

From our own history, we can see that labels can be used to refer to people, especially due to their ethnic or other background. The abolition of slavery in America in the aftermath of the Civil War brought poor Whites in conflict with an ethnic group, Blacks, who vied for the same economic and other opportunities. But we need to take a step back and appreciate that this same scenario operates across the world as a way of keeping opportunities available for some over others. Everyone carries out a similar modus operandi, that is, a way of operating, within their lives, be this for their kith and kin, or using some other criterion to make the determination for who is in and who is out as related above.

If we return to Israel and Hamas, the Israelis require military service from their citizens in order to receive government benefits. Some Jews, typically those who identify as "religious," opt out of military service and so are not eligible for such benefits. Some religious Jews, however, do perform such service, and the government grants them some accommodations so that they can remain observant during their military service. Palestinians do not qualify, because they are not citizens of Israel. Nonetheless, these two groups had co-existed for a time, though that co-existence developed into periodic attacks on Israel through suicide bombers and the like, which served to destabilize Israel. Israel would counter such attacks by shelling known Hamas strongholds. Israel "tolerated" these attacks to some extent, but then found that these policies went nowhere toward lessening the attacks. They then installed an enormous wall between Israel and Gaza, condemning the Palestinians to lives virtually dictated by Israel. The Palestinians have thus paid the price for Hamas' engagement in violence as it occurs today.

Clarity?

The death toll of citizens in Gaza has surpassed 20,000, as Israel also reports that it has killed more than 2,000 Hamas fighters. No one can know the precise figures. Israel recently reported that it mistakenly killed many Palestinians due to miscommunication. It has even killed its own freed hostages. It has further decimated Gaza through its systematic bombing. Jewish citizens of the West Bank, extremist even by the standards of their fellow Israelites, have taken up arms against the Palestinians who have lived there for centuries, even occupying their land, which has been a sticking point for decades, even among Jews. The army is complicit with these settlers, as is Prime Minister Netanyahu. Where will it end?

Covid

Covid served as a time for soul-searching, but instead people continued to harbor their anger, prejudices, resentments, and other narratives that paint their actions as right or even righteous over the actions of others. People tend to accentuate that their actions are justified, no matter how they operate. Problems develop, however, when people do not fight their own battles, but instead rely upon others to carry this out as proxies. This is where peace stands in between two opposing forces, but represents neither, yet must be respected by both sides so that they can move forward.

Church of the Holy Sepulcher

Christians steeped in liturgical traditions make claims on the Church of the Holy Sepulcher, the holiest place in all of Christendom, located in Jerusalem. Yet, they can't agree on much of anything and commonly come to fisticuffs about the slightest issue. A Muslim family maintains the key to the church itself, since the Christian groups play favorites. In other words, religious people are no better or worse than those who engage in secular affairs, which doesn't say much, except negatively, in what these groups espouse. They have their own agendas which they attempt to promote.

From my own study of religion, the quest for peace in religious terms is as problematic as that promoted in secular terms. Instead, both must carry with them that the simple cessation of arms is insufficient to realize peace if the aggression that leads to the violence innate to the human condition is not also addressed.

War in General

Israel is pulverizing Gaza, whereas Hamas is holding Israeli hostages, though Israel also holds Palestinians hostage, though the news reports these people as "prisoners." The difference in terminology is remarkable. The grave error on Israel's side of killing its own citizens underscores how little Israeli soldiers can take actions without their leadership's guidance. But it also demonstrates a grave communication difficulty between command and the front line. The Israeli command's propaganda arm has recently taken responsibility for the army's actions, as it now identifies when it engages in so-called immoral actions or other war crimes. But this is war. People wish to see a "fair" war take place, but that is impossible. Israel has the backing of the US, who, in effect, is saying, "Don't kill civilians, just kill Hamas," as though war is a calculable, black-and-white undertaking. It is not. Such initiatives do, however, score political points. Even in the midst of so much suffering, politicians capitalize on the situation. This demonstrates how sad the entire situation really is.

Deterrence

Israel has its "Iron Dome" that protects it from aerial assaults, especially in the midst of so many Arab nations that question its right to exist. It has a great fighting force to defend itself. It has actually held back the full brunt of its weaponry for a long time. It is now taking its fight to the ground, provoked by the attack on 7 October. The people of Israel never envisioned that they would be engaging in a pogrom against the Palestinians, yet that is what it is. We've seen images of Palestinians in their underwear being interrogated. Other atrocities will come to light over time. Some politicians suggest that Israel is waging a "righteous" war. There are no righteous wars or attacks. There is only aggression that, unless it is rechanneled, will manifest itself, typically through violent means. No one is immune. Is Israel justified? Yes. Should it be engaging in the intensity of attacks that it is? That is a different question. But with the US behind it, there is little holding it back. The US serves as a strong deterrent behind the scenes that others ought not interfere, but we don't see Egypt opening up its borders to fleeing Palestinians, despite their religious or other connections. Does this sound familiar?

Peace of a Different Sort

People are manifesting their violent tendencies in this country against Jews and others. But I am hesitant, as related above, to believe that just Jews are being targeted, which even television ads admit. Instead, I believe that people are focusing their aggression on the vulnerable in general. I have related about passive racism above. If there is someone who fits the bill as someone who is different, then this person or group of persons will be targeted.

I do not believe that "training" related to various forms of hatred helps to deal with aggression. It merely redirects it, if it does even this. Such training, however, does not deal with the aggression itself. It is from such an appreciation that I understand sports, drama, and other programs that can help students to re-channel their energies in general, so that they can lead happier and more productive lives. However, appreciation for this redirection or re-channeling as well as acknowledging innate aggression, must work in tandem. In particular, I do not discount the place of martial arts for helping young people to channel their aggression in helpful ways. I believe that we attempt to paper over difficult circumstances, when they are at the heart of the problem.

Aggression and Its Consequences

Peace must have at its core the ability to contend with one's own hurt feelings, as well as those that develop from the inability to do what one wants to do, which are typically anger and resentment. These can become catchalls for many people, especially young men. Some people have adopted the posture that their hurt or negative feelings constitute a reason for engaging in a violent act against another. Such individuals may not have been taught about or otherwise invited to engage in emotional regulation. Nonetheless, by an underlying current of society pushing the notion that people should not have aggression, we are placing ourselves between a rock and a hard place. Aggression is a part of the human condition that people must contend with on an individual basis, but group activities can help to redirect aggression into something helpful and meaningful. Every religious faith that I am aware of acknowledges the presence of such aggression. The question is, however, how to deal with it.

Soldier On

One obvious way of channeling aggression is through martial arts, but another parallel way is through military service.[31] Recognizing the impact

---

[31] I appreciate the complex network of skills that mixed martial artists have. I enjoy watching Ultimate Fighting Championship (UFC) precisely because of this. There are some fighters who present themselves as thugs. There are others, however, who are truly artists in that they bring to bear boxing, grappling, kicking, and other strategies to meet their opponent. They have channeled their aggression and demonstrate self-mastery. An incident during a Congressional hearing recently occurred, where a former Mixed Martial Arts (MMA) fighter, now a member of Congress, threatened a person who testified, who had allegedly disrespected him on social media. The Week Staff, "Congress: Why Are GOP Lawmakers Threatening Violence?" *The Week*, December 1, 2023, p. 6.

of one's actions within "messy" circumstances that can have severe implications can help to bring the consequences of actions into reality for many people. I have never served in the military, though I have had interactions with many service men and women, particularly Chaplains. I envision that the harsh realities that military members encounter can change their lives forever as they witness and experience peoples' hatreds and murderous behavior, depending, of course, on where they are stationed. Members of law enforcement must encounter similar sorts of circumstances. But not everyone will serve in the military or law enforcement, and this is only one direction for peace, though it is a vital one to protect another kind of peace, which comes from within.

"If You Want Peace, …"

"If you want peace, work for justice." These words of Dr. Martin Luther King, Jr., underscore that some part of a lack of peace stems from the injustices that can occur within one's own country. This is certainly true, and this can be a call to action for groups to address problems in earnest. But such an issue can also stem from the unwillingness of some to take responsibility for their own actions and act accountably.

I detailed above how a lack of accountability can stand in the way of advancing society in positive ways. But such an approach starts with the individual. If I am walking along and hit by a car by someone and injured, then this is someone else's fault. Nonetheless, I'm the one who needs to address the fact of my injuries in the manner in which I can do so. In general, when we look at situations and develop methods for addressing those concerns, then we can move from victimhood to responsibility to taking action. Such a way of moving forward does not exonerate the other party from having hit me. I may still pursue a law suit against that individual, but I must also rise to the occasion and do what I believe is right, work toward my own health, growth, and development *despite the actions of the other*. We can often get distracted to such an extent by others that we fail to act ourselves.

---

https://usmagazine.theweek.com/full_page_image/the-week-us-2023-12-01-page-6/content.html.

I have to admit that I once had the occasion to teach that, no matter what someone's upbringing may have been—good or bad or some combination, which is most typical—people as individuals are still responsible for ensuring that they get the help that they need. I was called on the carpet for making such a claim, yet I do believe it. This does not preclude asking others for assistance to address one's needs or otherwise achieve one's goals. But it does mean that I have to ask for that help, taking responsibility to its logical conclusion. Responsibility from my perspective, then, can lead a person toward an internal type of peace that does not depend on the actions of others, but instead appreciates one's own integrity, mettle, character, or some other word to convey the sense of an internal center. This is the site of inner peace.

Inner Peace

From my perspective, accepting oneself is the source of true peace. It means a state of balance in one's life, where a person accepts him or herself as *valued* and *valuable*, and acting from such a center, recognizing one's flaws and strengths. Recognizing such a state of being does not occur over night. It happens within the crucible of one's heart and soul, where a person establishes boundaries with others, so as to develop a sense of self on one's own. This takes years to develop, and it is seemingly in constant flux, but when a person can identify a "zone" within oneself that that person appreciates as "me" and then acts from this place. This metaphor is the lens through which I view inner peace. I suggest that the process requires internal conflict to "build" such a "sacred" space, and only those willing to undertake such a "mission" will discover this type of peace.

Yet, I would suggest that this process is the key to formulating a plan for peace that is more comprehensive than a religious tradition or political party or some other affiliation. Such understandings can be helpful, but they pale in comparison when placed side by side with the essence of one's sense of self understood in such a way. I have infrequently met such individuals who recognize themselves and thus peace within themselves. I can attest, however, that they do exist. They serve as sources of peace, which emanates from their core, which shine like rays within their fields of influence. Their effect is almost without limit.

Lack of Peace

But I also find individuals who have not dealt with their inner "demons," who bring forward a lack of peace by their unwillingness to contend with their inner selves. They bring chaos and destruction to situations and to people in the counter-effect developed above. I mention such individuals not to condemn them, but to appreciate that this is the reason we must still maintain forces to deal with such individuals as we also invite them to obtain the help that they need. By refusing or otherwise not knowing how to deal with their inner turmoil, these individuals can inflict grave harm on others. I would suggest that the overly optimistic tendency to view everyone in positive terms can backfire in significant ways, because not everyone is willing to contend with their darkness, and there can be significant implications for others who enter their ambit.

Conclusion

The discussion of peace took us from present conflicts to a recognition of our own ability to inflict harm on others, especially when we do not deal with our own aggressive natures. Such an understanding helped us to recognize that we must contend with our darkness and the circumstances that we meet, so that we can "know" peace within ourselves, but also so that we can bring it about by our actions, flowing from our inner state. Inner peace is not realized overnight. It takes time literally to wrestle within ourselves with the matters that cause us upset. Nonetheless, we are ourselves responsible for getting the help that we need if we meet impasses. Such a program stems from a radical sense of accountability. Unless we take responsibility for our actions at a personal level, we will not become true individuals. Embracing a false sense of individuality can lead to becoming enslaved to the systems in which we find ourselves, believing that we are not led and guided by the circumstances in which we find ourselves. This is a fallacy. The people around us can determine our trajectory. A sense of inner self, however, can help a person to make the appropriate decision to follow the crowd or go one's own way, and everything in between. Peace means a lack of coercion must be brought to bear, so that people can work together to formulate plans that benefit both the individual and others, without people wondering why Johnny or Mary got a bigger cookie. Instead, larger concerns loom on the horizon, but unless people rise to meet such concerns from a place of relative peace, then we are doomed to repeat the same back and forth meanderings that may serve as “solutions” for the moment, but will not have lasting value or efficacy. Unless we come from such a state of being, one that involves trust, we will continue to play games. I enjoy games, but I get tired of them. Instead, my hope is that we can work toward respecting each other and engaging with one another, so that we can make forward strides and concerted efforts. If this does not happen, then I am fearful about where the current aggression will take us, given that many deny that it is there in the first place. This can only add to its power over people.

APPENDIX A: DEALING WITH AGGRESSION

There is no sure-fire way to deal with aggression, except by training it, which can lead to rechanneling it, but this starts first with acknowledging it. I would suggest the following approach, which can help parents and children—which is where such training begins—to address aggression in its many forms.

From Secular to Transcendent

"From secular to transcendent" has to do with how people become ensconced in their particular realities, whatever these may be. This is not a bad thing necessarily, but saying this, for some, implies that it is a good thing, and that is also not true. It just is what it is. This is the nature of what is required in society in general, that is, to move from the secular to the transcendent. It is an attitudinal shift, which may acknowledge God, but it has to do with more than just that. It must also acknowledge the practical aspects of one's life together with one's capacity or capacities. I offer a hypothetical situation.

If someone watches television or plays video games or is otherwise enmeshed in one's smartphone for excessive amounts of time, which means that these things impede one's academic or social or emotional or spiritual progress, then it is time to re-examine one's use of them. Parents must take the lead in their children's lives to identify boundaries in the use of such devices. In effect, these are passive engagements that do not translate well into real-life skills. Many believe that the best approach to stop these practices is to stop using these devices altogether and go "cold turkey." I do not agree. This can and probably will produce resentment. Given that most people must use at least some of these devices for work, which will not change over time, persons must recognize their own legitimate use and go from there.

But to stop usage all at once will not work over time. The same problem exists for dieting, stopping bad habits, beginning good habits, and a host of other things that people wish to start or end. In other words, *practice makes permanent.* People in the technical age have adapted their lives to accommodating technology to such an extent that it can impinge upon growth and development as human persons. It does not have to do so. Many uses of technology are beneficial. Many, however, are detrimental to people's growth.

In relating these comments, I am underscoring that people use technology and they enjoy doing so or they would not do it. We can cast aspersions at companies for making video games addictive and others for using people's search history to sell you things, but the fact is that people need to grow and develop their inner selves, otherwise they will be susceptible to such mindless operations. They will not be able to overcome much of anything in their lives without breaking free, but this means developing or uncovering the nature of freedom that resides within each of us, but it must be acknowledged, developed, and strengthened, otherwise we will go nowhere.

The theologian Paul Tillich recognized a difference between *freedom from* and *freedom for. Freedom from* is when someone gains the ability no longer to be, in effect, chained to something—an addiction or bad habit or the like. On the other side of this development is the *freedom for*, that is, the ability then to do something else. I believe that this is where most of our present systems fail us. We must live in the realm of *freedom from* for a time admittedly, but then we must cross over to *freedom for.* This is a difficult transition to make, because it puts us in the no-man's land of having to learn some behavior or encounter some subject, which can be difficult to do. What we seldom speak about, however, is appreciating the emotional impact that we feel or otherwise associate with whatever we are attempting to gain *freedom from.* We wouldn't be doing it, unless it had some positive experience for us, though I also believe that we might keep falling back into it because we may lack alternatives for moving forward.

In general, people become addicted or habituated to something, because they did not pursue another trajectory that could deliver pleasure or satisfaction or fulfillment in some other way, so they constantly return to the one source (addiction), because they have nothing else to turn to. This is a simplistic rendering of addiction, and I wish not to understate people's struggles with addictions. Nonetheless, they might "get clean" (*freedom from*), but then, because they never developed other pursuits, they fall back into the addiction, because there is no *freedom for*. For example, you may work hard to land a job—getting all of the requirements accomplished and finally getting the job. You have *freedom from* joblessness, but now you have to rise to the occasion and learn and perform the job—*freedom for*. Unless you do the job, you won't develop the capacity to realize its impact on your life, which all jobs have the potential for doing, but our capacity or openness to something can determine how much we gain from our employment.

Job, Career, Vocation

I've had many jobs in my life. Many served as employment to obtain money, so that I could realize other pursuits or goals, like going to college or saving for something that I wanted. But jobs can also provide opportunities to gain skills. But if we are so concerned with the money end of the job, then we can lose the inner sense of what jobs have to offer. If we don't recognize, in effect, what even the lowliest of jobs can deliver for us and to us, then we will be focused solely on the money and never grow because of whatever job that we have. Once again, resentment can develop.

When it comes to viewing a job as a career, we *do* recognize what the job can do for us, and we set out to obtain those skills and grow because of them. We may be able to "see ourselves" performing that job for years and years. We become good at the job and we can see that there was an exchange that took place. Over time, we learned the ropes and may have even become an expert at the job. If we use the same skills and keep ourselves open to growth, then we might be able to view the course of our jobs as a career, which is more than simply a job, but something that has demonstrable markers that point to a journey of developing skills and expertise. This is at a different level.

When it comes to a vocation, this is where people throw themselves into whatever it is. First-responders must, by the nature of their work, throw themselves into their work. It is a vocation, which fully encompasses the person who performs it. People in the medical field or ministry must do the same. Some have moved away from this level of involvement, wishing to accomplish their life's goals through different means, but they will probably be restless and unhappy, given that such individuals are meant to devote their whole selves to such endeavors. But how does this relate to our discussion?

Trial and Error

We've become a society that is wired so tightly that we lose the purpose behind trial and error, which is endemic to the human condition. We believe that we need to have figured everything out within our lives, rather than that it is a learning experience. Instead, society has assumptions built in within it that can take their toll. For instance, testing in elementary, middle, and high school can be helpful, so that teachers know which children are struggling with reading or math. Earlier interventions of whatever sort deliver better and more long-lasting results over time. But we have an unrealistic expectation that schools will deliver for children in overarching ways, because there is a national mandate for education. But what about parents?

Parents, too, need to stimulate their children to learn at home, but learning should be understood beyond the realm of simply academics. Parents model behaviors for dealing with situations for their children, which they will, in turn, pick up, either actively or passively. Such lessons are just as important as academic ones—probably even more so. If, instead, parents rely on electronic devices to teach children these important human lessons, then they will have failed their children.[32] Schools must deliver for

[32] See Eloise Hendy, "When Kids are Shaped by Screens," *The Week*, December 8, 2023, p. 12. https://usmagazine.theweek.com/full_page_image/the-week-us-2023-12-08-page-12/content.html.

children, but parents ought to do so, as well. This is not to say that parents are given blueprints for how to deal with their children, but parents should recognize their place in their children's lives and not try to avoid it.

Parents Play a Different Role

Parents do not have the same role as a teacher or principal in a school. Parents are parents. They do not have the role of a friend. What I have found is that parents do not appreciate that parent as parent is a distinctive role. We tend to gravitate toward roles that we already know, rather than learn something about a new one. This is again a part of the human condition tending toward the least common denominator. We most often take the path of least resistance.

But parenting is by its nature a vocation, where parents need to throw themselves into it wholeheartedly. If they hold back, then their children will recognize this and they will take advantage—as all children do—of the lack of a role-model to follow, but also to misbehave given the lack of oversight. Parents are, in effect, undermining how their children handle aggression, since children will pout and then move toward technology to assuage their bad feelings. Parents can assign a time-out, which identifies a boundary and a difficulty with children's behavior, but I find that time-outs, though politically correct, are largely ineffective for teaching children to adapt their aggressive behavior, as society now demonstrates. A real punishment, which may or may not be corporal, ensures that the lesson is learned. (I am not advocating abuse of any sort!) But when parents effectively convey boundaries and have their children "sit with it," then they are demonstrating their love for them into the future, since such lessons will be lifelong and enduring.

Chores

Some US children have a great deal of free time. This can be a good thing, but it can also be detrimental. Keeping children busy with substantive things to do, like chores, can help them to focus their energies in productive, useful ways, which is helpful for channeling energy, which is not always aggression, but which can go in that direction through a mood swing, especially for adolescents. Assigning chores and verifying that they have been accomplished—which is critical—helps children to develop responsibility and accountability. If they don't learn such things in the home, where else will they learn them? Parents who do everything for their children—and I know some—may have issues with control and perfectionism. They need to permit messiness to occur. Messiness is by nature not pretty. On most occasions, "good enough" is sufficient, but can parents tolerate the messiness? That's the question. Schools can bring about some of this important learning, but if parents don't demonstrate that they care about school work and learning in general, then the lessons taught at school will be lost. All lessons, no matter who is performing them, require follow-up and follow-through, at least at some level, to ensure that the lesson is being received, if not learned. Parents who presume that their children are completing their homework or chores are setting themselves up for disappointment and not taking their responsibility as parents seriously. Parents are not their children's friends. They have a different role to play. If parents do not "stake out" what that role is from the outset, then children may dominate their parents. This is a worst-case scenario.

Group Activities

I hated group activities as a child, where we should distinguish groups from family, which I otherwise enjoyed, given that I have a large family. Nonetheless, group interactions help children to adapt to or at least see societal norms in action. Eating with other people is a great way to witness how people interact, that is, speak, engage socially, and otherwise observe decorum. This can speak volumes, but it requires feedback. Most people do what they do and move on; they do not recognize how their actions interact within a broader spectrum of behaviors, unless someone points this out to them. This is why parents who are cognizant of others' needs and social conventions can help their children to fit in. What child is going to land a job if he or she cannot sit still or otherwise speak in an articulate manner? Parents need to take the lead in ensuring that their children can function within a group, but can also benefit from it. Parents should listen closely to their children's speech patterns and other behaviors. I suppose that it's hard to spot difficulties that require a professional, but a speech impediment, like a stutter, or problem walking, needs invention sooner rather than later.

In education, I've heard it repeated: "Learn to read and read to learn," which means that we learn how to read, so that, through reading, we can gain knowledge and learn more. Reading is the vehicle for learning. Group activities are the vehicle for learning social skills by practicing them. Boy Scouts and Girl Scouts are groups that foster developing goals for children, as they must also interact with others. Sports, band, and drama can help as well, though band and drama can also appear to be group activities, but if children do not practice instruments or otherwise interact with others in these groups, then they can lose the benefit of the group activity. Children need to be encouraged in their activities, completing them a little at a time, but they must also be checked in their delivery of milestones along the way. By parents taking interest in their children along the way, they demonstrate that they care, so that children can come to them with greater problems later on, recognizing that they can trust their parents. If parents do not do this and they believe that their children will confide in them, then they are living in a dream world, setting their children up for possible future failures because their children won't know where to turn.

Other Appropriate Activities

Children will typically follow their parents in engaging in activities. These are good things. Such hobbies offer children opportunities from which to draw. They may or may not enjoy them. At least, however, they have a basis in something from which to choose. Again, drawing from society's inability to tolerate trial and error, there is nothing wrong with not knowing what to do with one's time, but parents ought to direct their children to find something to do, which does not involve technology. Technology is the easy way out, it seems to me, but a recommendation to read a book or write in a journal or go play outside or phone a friend are all things that children can do which can prove helpful for them to expand their horizons. In a society that has so much, it seems as though we have become shockingly self-absorbed, so that we do not mix with others, unless exceptionally. This is problematic. Unless we open ourselves to the outside world, we will remain limited within our perceptions, so that we do not grow and might even engage in delusional thinking, which is any thinking that cannot stand scrutiny by others and reality itself.

All of us need to practice sharing what we are thinking with others, so that we do not implode or otherwise believe that we are the source of all reality. We are not. By assisting children in dealing with their inner lives, especially their aggression, parents can foster their growth into the future. This, it seems to me, as developed above, is the best “gift” or “legacy” that they can leave to their children. If they do not accomplish this, then, no matter what the financial situation parents will have left to their children, they will in actuality have left them in a state of poverty. Such a state of being leaves their future in the hands of others who may not care about them. This is a clear-cut recipe for disaster, which could have been avoided.

Mindfulness

In order for people to break free from “group think” or the collective in a manner that still respects the collective, but also the individual, I believe that developing a sense of self is imperative, but this involves dealing with one’s own racing thoughts or the unconscious in general. Mindfulness is the term for a method of meditation that can serve as a means for recognizing these racing thoughts, which can at least partially dissipate if people devote themselves to this practice on a regular, that is, daily, basis.

Mindfulness is the ability to “rest with oneself.” It is a state between being fully awake and asleep, which is why people who begin the practice tend to fall asleep at the beginning of the practice. But for those who persevere, it is a way of centering oneself within the cacophony of one’s thoughts, so that one can find a way through to permit one’s self to emerge “above the fray.” Active engagement with pressing matters is important, such as wrestling with ethical or moral dilemmas, which different people face at varying levels of engagement. But these are active thought processes. I have heard of people who, for instance, in sports, picture in their minds what they are going to do on the playing field. I suppose that picturing such scenarios can be beneficial. I do not possess the ability to carry out such an undertaking. Nonetheless, such an ego-based process is also not what I am talking about. Mindfulness is between passive and active thoughts, which is why it can be so effective. A possible scenario might serve to illustrate this practice better.

Queeziness

Have you ever had to stand up in front of people and make a presentation or otherwise speak before superiors? You know that "knot" or queeziness that you get in your stomach, especially the first time that you had to do it? I will try to explain how that comes about using a metaphor.[33]

When we experience that knot, I propose that we are following the mistaken belief that our performance during that speech somehow implicates our identity, so, when we believe that we will be criticized, we believe that our identity, that which makes us who we are, is going to be attacked. We must gradually confront this mistaken belief, because it is not true. We are not necessarily what we do, though our activities at work or other occupations over a period of time *can* form us. But, in general, just because we receive a failing grade on a paper or flunk a driving test *doesn't mean that we are failures*. If you believe this, then it's time to recognize that your value is innate; it does not come necessarily from your actions or someone else's assessment of you. The knot or sting that you experience is associating your identity with whatever it is that you are doing and for which you may receive criticism.

We are all aware of the saying: "Sticks and stones may break my bones, but names will never hurt me." The problem is that, unless we've considered these words in earnest, that is, *truly taken them to heart*, all of us come from a place of insecurity, where names, that is, criticism, *can* hurt us, which means *emotionally* hurt us. We do not need to follow such a lead. Instead, by observation and mindfulness, people can overcome such knots or stings within themselves, not so much so that they become impervious to them, but instead, because they rise above them. They can take them in stride. This is actually strengthening one's interior value, that is, one's identity and ego-strength. When we accomplish this, we have made the words about names not hurting us become real, that is, entering the reality of ourselves. By constantly observing our own reactions to such criticism, instead of running from them or denying them, we can make

---

[33] For the best account that I have read that details the exchange between one's inner and outer selves, see W. Timothy Gallwey, *The Inner Game of Tennis: The Classic Guide to the Mental Side of Peak Performance* (New York: Random House, 1974; 2008).

progress in developing interior strength, which is actually a strengthening of how people view themselves, their identity.

The Sting of Criticism

When people want to be mean, they will oftentimes be critical, which they know can be painful for another person—that's why they do it! But one's attitude can determine how criticism is taken and appreciated.

If we equate our identity with our feelings or our thoughts, then we could lose sight of the rest of what makes us human beings. If, instead, we recognize that feelings are one aspect of what makes a human who he or she is, then it will be easier to appreciate criticism's purpose: It can be seen as a way of becoming a better human being, as a coach would do for helping an athlete perform better. If, instead, it is seen as a mockery of who someone is, then it will be interpreted negatively; resentment will follow. Only people with sufficient ego-strength, that is, an interior sense of themselves as valuable, are able to recognize their need to become who they are right now through the help of others.

Peers and Friends

Having peers is more than having friends. Real friends want the best for the ones they care about, both now and in the future. A person has to be comfortable enough with him or herself, so that the person recognizes his or her own value, and in turn that person can help others to recognize their value. This is also a part of ego-strength. Those who take up a sport, I would suggest, for any duration, are willing to appreciate that a coach will call them out, so that the individual player improves both for himself or herself and for the team at large. It is a both-and scenario.

I would suggest that those adolescents who engage in video games or other behaviors for lengthy periods of time may not know what they want out of life for lack of ego-strength: They do not know their value, so they do not know what would help them to realize and actualize their potential, especially because they are getting little to no feedback from other peers or adults. Adolescents have trouble due to their age projecting out their futures, so these and other aspects conspire to limit their perspectives. The more that an adolescent is cognizant of his or her value through the development of ego-strength, which often involves making choices, the more that adolescent will be able to make coherent decisions about his or her betterment, though it may involve a timely question from another person, whether that person is a parent, a teacher, a coach, though also a peer.

In general, frustration can develop into aggression, because people do not know what they want, so, on the one hand, it becomes the catchall feeling of anger, which can turn outwardly into aggression or violence. If, on the other hand, we develop an opening through mindfulness for other options to make themselves known, then we can accommodate criticism and name-calling, because we recognize interiorly that we are more than what people say we are. Such a posture can deliver great rewards, but people generally fall into the trap of believing other people's comments about them. Instead, the "mindful" person can evaluate the relative merit of others' comments. For example, someone might call me an idiot. I am an idiot at times, that's for sure. But when someone calls me one, can I recognize whether I am at the moment? Self-knowledge will determine my reactions, together with objectivity about myself and recognizing my own value. All of these go hand-in-hand.

Conclusion

Developing ego-strength, fostering mindfulness, and observing one's internal states can develop over time, so that people come at things from an established center. If, instead, we are de-centered, then we may feel off-kilter if people confront us. Instead, when we recognize our true identity and value, such a realization can ensure that we view ourselves in a healthy and constructive way. This does not eliminate confrontations. It merely gives us a way of appreciating our value, as it also gives us the ability to look at things from a more objective perspective. Objectivity is helpful for appreciating most things in life. The confluence of developed ego-strength, mindfulness, and the ability to observe can help to ensure that we grow in a manner that helps us to become our true selves. Most people can be idiots at times—I know that I can. But this need not be our primary identity. Instead, by recognizing our true identity, we can become who we were meant to be and realize a future that helps us to bring potential into reality.

BIBLIOGRAPHY

A Few Good Men. Directed by Rob Reiner. Columbia Pictures. 1992. https://en.wikipedia.org/wiki/A_Few_Good_Men. Last updated 7 March 2024.

Arrival. Directed by Denis Villeneuve. Paramount Pictures. 2016. https://en.wikipedia.org/wiki/Arrival_(film). Last updated 13 March 2024.

Baltimore Examiner Staff. "Baltimore Homicides: A 5-Year Analysis." *Baltimore Examiner*. December 25, 2023. https://www.baltimoreexaminer.com/baltimore-homicides/.

Catholic News Service. "Like 5th Circuit, 8th Circuit Strikes Down Biden's Transgender Mandate." *The Pilot*, 20 December 22. https://www.thebostonpilot.com/article.php?ID=193779.

Debczak, Michele. "These Revised Guidelines Redefine Birth Years and Classifications for Millennials, Gen Z, and Gen Alpha." *Mental*

Floss, Dec. 6, 2019; updated Mar. 10, 2023. https://www.mentalfloss.com/article/609811/age-ranges-millennials-and-generation-z.

Dilanian, Ken. "Most People Think the U.S. Crime Rate is Rising. They're Wrong." *NBCNews*, Dec. 16, 2023. https://www.nbcnews.com/news/us-news/people-think-crime-rate-up-actually-down-rcna129585.

Evans, Murray. "State Supreme Court Denies Walters' 2nd Bid to Intervene in Catholic Charter School Suit." *The Oklahoman*, Dec. 18, 2023. https://www.oklahoman.com/story/news/education/2023/12/18/walters-intervention-in-catholic-charter-school-case-denied-again/71967304007/.

Follman, Mark. "What Drives Mass Shooters to Kill." *The Week*, June 3, 2022, p. 12.

Fry, Edward. *1000 Instant Words: The Most Common Words for Teaching Reading, Writing, and Spelling*. Unk. pub. 1999.

Gallwey, W. Timothy. *The Inner Game of Tennis: The Classic Guide to the Mental Side of Peak Performance*. New York: Random House, 1974; 2008.

Gladwell, Malcolm. *The Tipping Point: How Little Things Can Make a Big Difference*. New York: Little, Brown and Company, 2002.

Hendy, Eloise. “When Kids are Shaped by Screens.” *The Week*, December 8, 2023, p. 12. https://usmagazine.theweek.com/full_page_image/the-week-us-2023-12-08-page-12/content.html.

Lindsay, Patrick. *Make the Most of You: 170 Ways to be the Best You Can*. New York: MJF Books, 2015.

Lovett, Samuel. “Tavistock Gender Clinic Facing Legal Action Over ‘Failure of Care’ Claims.” *The Independent*, 11 August 2022. https://www.independent.co.uk/news/health/tavistock-gender-clinic-lawyers-latest-b2143006.html.

Montenaro, Domenico. “What Does the Word ‘Woke’ Really Mean, and Where Does It Come From?” *National Public Radio* (NPR), July 19, 2023. https://www.npr.org/2023/07/19/1188543449/what-does-the-word-woke-really-mean-and-where-does-it-come-from.

The Chronicles of Riddick. Directed by David Twohy. Universal Pictures. 2004. https://en.wikipedia.org/wiki/The_Chronicles_of_Riddick_(franchise). Last updated 7 March 2024.

The Week Staff. "Congress: Why Are GOP Lawmakers Threatening Violence?" *The Week*, December 1, 2023, p. 6. https://usmagazine.theweek.com/full_page_image/the-week-us-2023-12-01-page-6/content.html.

The Week Staff. "Health and Science." *The Week*, Nov. 3, 2023, p. 21. https://usmagazine.theweek.com/full_page_image/the-week-us-2023-11-03-page-20/content.html.

The Week Staff. "Viewpoint." *The Week*, July 8/July 15, 2022, p. 12.

U. S. Congress. Individuals with Disabilities Education Act (IDEA). Pub. L. 101-476. 2004. https://sites.ed.gov/idea/about-idea/.

U. S. Congress. No Child Left Behind Act (NCLB) of 2001, P.L. 107-110, 20 U.S.C. § 6319 (2002). https://www.congress.gov/bill/107th-congress/house-bill/1.

U. S. Department of Education. Every Student Succeeds Act (ESSA). 2015. https://www.ed.gov/essa?src%3Drn.

U. S. District Court, *Flores v. Arizona*, 1992. https://azleg.gov/legtext/47leg/2r/summary/h.hb2064_02-27-06_astransmittedtogovernor.doc.htm.

U. S. Supreme Court. *Carson v. Makin*, 2022. https://www.law.cornell.edu/supct/cert/20-1088.

U. S. Supreme Court. *Lau v. Nichols*, 1974. https://supreme.justia.com/cases/federal/us/414/563/.

U. S. Supreme Court. *Mast vs. Fillmore County*, 2021. https://www.law.cornell.edu/supremecourt/text/20-7028.

U. S. Supreme Court. *Plyer v. Doe*, 1982. https://www.law.cornell.edu/wex/plyler_v_doe.

U. S. Supreme Court. *Roe v. Wade*, 1972. https://supreme.justia.com/cases/federal/us/410/113/.

U. S. Supreme Court. *United States v. Virginia et al.*, 1996. https://library.law.hawaii.edu/2017/01/23/united-states-v-virginia-case-summary/.

www.ingramcontent.com/pod-product-compliance
Lightning Source LLC
LaVergne TN
LVHW010604160826
845677LV00013B/3236